Go Global Leadership Keys

Dr. Kelafo Collie, M.D.
Shallaywa Collie, MBA

GO Global Leadership Keys

Strategies for Your Business, Brand, and Organization to Have Global Impact

ISBN 978-1-7355413-3-4

www.shallaywa.com Published by:

Majestic Priesthood Publication, Freeport, Grand Bahama, Bahamas.

Email: mpppublications@gmail.com

1-242-727-2137

Printed in the United States of America

Contents

Foreword

I GREW UP IN THE street of Nassau, The Bahamas in a home with 10 other people, including grandparents, mother and her siblings. God has taken that little boy to all over North America, the Caribbean, all through Africa and Southeast Asia. More so, our organization; Kingdom Apostolic Ministry and Kingdom Apostolic Global Network is in every one of those nations. We have trained, equipped and sent out thousands of leaders who have positively influenced the world.

In addition, we have helped many other leaders write to books, and by the special grace of God, TBN and Preach the Word Network featured us. We are currently on Kingdom Insight, Dominion TV, and Power and Glory TV (www.powerandglorytv.tv). Therefore, for the past few years, we have prepared ourselves for the digital change. Literarily, we have done thousands of teaching, training and developing. You can see more on our web page and Facebook page. You would see some of the things we have done. We could not capture all of the moments, but we have tried to capture as many as we could.

In this book, we will share the secrets that we have learnt. We have been privileged to sit at the feet of many great men and women who have gone into the world, have taken their organization, ministry, books, CDs, teachings and gifts into the world, and have been tremendously blessed. We want to give you that same opportunity.

First, we want to let you know that you have great abilities. Every person has God-given gifts, skills and ability. The Bible says, *"The Lord gives gifts and callings without repentance"* (Romans 11:29). This means that everyone created by God has a gift. You might not be a lawyer or doctor but a stay-at-home mom, a cook or an artist; you may be a person who can sing or write books and you have the dreams of producing a bestselling book. People from different nations are reading the books that my wife and I wrote. Television programs feature us on the same platform as Dr. Bill Winston, Kenneth Copeland, and Pastor Rod Parsley on Dominion TV on a daily basis. We are honored, and I am saying that to let you know that we all have something in one way or the other to contribute to the world.

Dr. Kelafo Z. Collie, M.D.

PREFACE

The 8 M's Of Global Influence

INFLUENCE IS A POWERFUL tool when purpose drives it. Having desire for influence is not bad; but do you have a purpose for it? What do you hope to accomplish with this influence? How will you manage this influence? It could be that you just want to be influential just for the feeling. It could be that you have a dream of your books, tapes, CDs, organization or company being global and having global clients. It could be that you see yourself traveling to these nations and visiting these places because you have a heart for people. It could be that you want to explore other places of the world. This is the "why" of your influence. The "why" talks about the things you will do when you get to the seat of influence.

Take 60 seconds to think about why you exist and why you want to do the things in your heart. The world has changed, but why are you changing? Why are you restructuring your life? Why are you resetting your dreams and your aspirations? The answer to these thoughts-provoking questions points to the 'why' of your influence. The 8 M's of global influence is for people who are ready to use the technology, science, their gifts, and skills.

1. Mission

According to the English Dictionary, Mission is a set of tasks that fulfills a purpose or duty. Mission is very important to influence. Influential people are mission-driven. What is your mission? What are you born to do? What impact are you 'called' to make?

What do you want to do? Without a vision, you will perish. Without a clear mission statement of who you are, what you are about, where you are going, whom you will take with you and which territory you should go, you cannot have influence. For instance, the mission of our organization is to impart the gospel to the world. We travel to touch lives, uplift people and leaders in places; this is our mission. We had a clear focus, we had a vision of it, we wrote that down. This is in the core of who we are, and all of a sudden, all of our energies and focus started moving in that direction.

2. Message

What is your message? What are you to say to the world? We have a challenge with many programs that we have seen out there, especially in leadership because not everyone is going to lead multi cooperation. Many people do not know that they have a message to the world. You do not need any special platform to share your message; you only need to identify what to say and where you find yourself.

You have 50 students that you can influence as a teacher. You are a nurse; you have hundreds of patients that cross your path or that you have to care for every month. Maybe you are a mom who takes care of the family, but the friends of your children are in your neighborhood as your audience. Your message is specific. If you have a book, your book must have a message.

What is the message you want to portray to the world? What is the message you want to portray about your life? It could be a book about your life, your personal story, your struggles towards overcoming challenges, you have a theological message, or you have a message of hope. You have a message of sharing what you have gone through. What exactly is your message? I want you to think about this.

Do you know without speaking a word your life is a message? When people think about you, what comes to their mind? What has your life been saying? What are your actions saying? People say that action speaks louder than words, and it is true. This is not to judge whatever your life said in the past, but you can change your life from today because you have a message.

3. Mandate

What is your mandate? Mandate is different from message. The mandate is, "What you engage in to advance the mission? The mandate is, "I have a personal response." For instance, if you have a mission to impart to children, then your mandate will be imparting children with great blessings using your life as a medium. Your mission could be to impart a change to the world for the glory of God and your mandate will be, "I want to encourage battered women." Your mandate ties with whatever your mission is.

4. Meat

Your meat is what you wake up with that consumes your being. When you get up in the morning, there are things you think about, but the meat of your life must be the thing that drives you. Jesus said, *"My meat is to do the will of my Father who sent me"* (John 4:34). He ate it, just as He ate three or four times a day. That is what He consumed Himself with every day. Just like how meat provides you with protein and fats and sometimes carbohydrates, and give energy, nourish the body and replenish the body. That is what your meat does to you. Jesus said, *"Man should not live by bread alone, but by every word that proceeded out of the mouth of God"* (Matthew 4:4).

In other words, Jesus is saying, "Your life is not what you eat; your life is the passion that drives you." The thing that characterized the passion or the drive you have is your meat. Jesus' passion drove Him to preach the gospel to the entire world. That became His food. When we get up in the morning, midday or nighttime that is what we do.

If something does not consume you, then it will be unbelievable to the world or people in the world; whether television, media, book writing or traveling in missions. We have gone to nations, and they do not accept us just because of what we say; they see it in us. They feel our passion. They sense our sincerity. They sense our love. Your meat really tells your integrity and sincerity. People are not concerned about your mission, mandate, message or meat until they can feel your sincerity. How do you do that? You just have to pray; spend time in the presence of the Lord. Ask this question, "Lord, what is the meat of my life in this season?" This lockdown should have brought us to the place where we asked the Lord, "What is our meat?"

5. Motivation

What is your motivation? What drives you? Different things drive different people. You could be in financial crisis, and the need to make money may be your motivation. The motivation for the book you are writing may be for funding. You want to write books because you want to be a best seller. Nothing is wrong with being a best seller. Nothing is wrong with having a bestselling book as a writer; because you want to sell 10,000 books, and out of that, you want to generate money to support your ministry, family or you want to write as a professional. There is nothing wrong with producing audio songs to go global, and to make it a full-time career. What is your motivation? It might be money, the joy of doing what you love or the feeling of satisfaction when you impart lives. We travel to different places to raise and inspire leadership in people. We wanted to see them arise and come into the fullness of their potentials. Your motivation might be that you just love people. Your motivation or your passion might be that you love children, you love women, you love men's ministry or you love cooking. Whatever your motivation, get it moving, and do not be ashamed or embarrassed about it.

6. Motto

You need to develop a life motto. As a leader on the path to global influence, you need a motto. A motto is a sentence or phrase that describes your life, purpose, and mandate. What is your motto? What is the thing you wake up to say about who you are? It can be something you read from a book or created for yourself.

Travelling to another country demands that you have your mission, message, mandate, meat, motivation, and motto in check. Sometimes, it took us 36 to 38 hours to travel to those countries. It takes two days to travel across Africa. You get there, you pour out, and then you have two days to return home. If we were not motivated, if we did not have a motto, if we did not have a mandate, when we arrive there, we would have been tired, lost, etc. It is a change of culture; it is a change of language. That is not only physically going to places, but it is also online. People are online, and they are hungry for the Word. This is why we get so discouraged in our spirit when we see people God has raised into places of influence using their platforms as a joke and a mockery.

The world will never respect the people of God if all they see is a bunch of comedians. At such a time as this, people need message, mission, motivation, and meat. We need to restore people. You need to develop these things before going online. The online platform is a very powerful tool, but many are unprepared and do not have a real message; they do not have a real passion or a mission. They do not have a motto that drives them. People are supposed to see you and say, "That man or woman, their motto in life is to love unconditionally, to help the helpless, or to be a friend to the poor." What did people call Jesus? Rabbi, Son of God, Son of man, Son of Mary, teacher, a friend of the publican, even the sinners had a name for Him. They identified Him with a specific quote that made Him special.

7. Mentor

To go global, restructuring your life for global impact is to have an uncommon, special mentor. We cannot tell you that we have done anything without special mentors. These people include some college friends, those we studied together with, who took us as a brother/sister and a friend. Mentors are uncommon people who either pray, encourage, stand by, and believe you. You need their support for global influence. You need them because when the lights and the cameras are off when you publish the book, the audio teaching gone viral, your message gone viral, you touch down on those nations that you wanted to go to, fed the hungry, and you started mission works in nations, they will be there to support and love you regardless.

You need people who believe in your heart, you need people who will pray you through, you need people who will stand with you to the end when everyone else look away because you are that man and woman that they saw in the light. You need uncommon mentors in your lives. If you do not have mentors in your life, you need to get some. Some of our mentors are alive, some have gone to be with the Lord. Even though they are gone, their books, tapes and CDs and their ministry still blesses our lives today.

8. Mentees

If you are going to influence the world, you need to mentor others. It is a spiritual principle. It is more blessed to give than to receive. Therefore, when we look at mentees, we should pour into their lives because we are called to sow good seeds. If it is more blessed to give than to receive, it automatically puts you in a position where you have to be a giver.

It automatically positions you for the blessing of Abraham. God told Abraham that He would bless him because he would teach his children and household. He also said He would bless Abraham and all the nations of the Earth through him. God chose Abraham not only because he was a man of faith; he is a channel through which nations are blessed.

As we travel about the world and reaching out to countless people, we commission, ordain and support leadership in different regions; we often wondered how God achieved such exploits through a little boy from Carmichael Road and a rural village.

However, the Lord said, "It's not just about you, it's because you have a heart to mentor others. You have a heart to serve." That is leadership, a call to serve!

Introduction

AT THE END OF Christ's assignment on earth, Jesus came to the disciples to address them and gave them the great commission. The Bible says,

> **"Therefore go and make disciples of all nations, baptizing them in the name of the Father and of the Son and of the Holy Spirit, and teaching them to obey everything I have commanded you. And surely I am with you always, to the very end of the age" (Mathew 28:19-20 NIV).**

We are not sent to a nation, but to nations. We are not to limit the scope of our assignments to our immediate environment, but look beyond to nations. Christ expects us to be revived and renewed in our mind, and not be limited by beliefs, traditions of men and individual weaknesses, so that we can advance the Kingdom of God in our diverse spheres of influence to nations of the world.

God's goal is to establish His Kingdom upon the earth. The Kingdom of God has to do with the glory, power, will and reign of God. God wants to decolonize the earth from the kingdom of darkness by bringing whoever accepts and submits to Him through Christ into the Kingdom of light. He desires to bring nations to enjoy salvation, satisfaction, and safety in Him.

Knowing that this is God's ultimate goal, as leaders in whatever capacities God has placed us, it is very important to know that we are God's instruments to achieve His agenda here on earth. The enemy also uses people to fulfill his evil goals, but as God's people, we must be willing and available to fulfill our part of the global agenda of God.

We are to teach all nations as Christ as instructed. As leaders, we realize Christ model for leadership remains the best, and we must not only practice this, we must also teach it. As entrepreneurs, our relationship with people should not only be transactional, but also transformational. The advent of digital technology and social media has influenced lots of things, thereby making it easier to be global influencers in leadership, ministry, and entrepreneurship. We should leverage on various platforms, tools and strategies to reach out to nations as the Lord instructs.

With the help of social media, we can see nations as classroom through which we are to teach the precepts, ordinances and excellence of God. We are sent into the cosmos, the system of the world, to bring in God's civilization. The Gospel is two winged; one is evangelism and the other is influence. The body of Christ has engaged evangelism so much that we forget that we are also sent to influence our world for God. Position yourself to influence the world as a kingdom leader and millionaire.

In this book, we shall look at various subjects as we journey towards becoming global leaders and entrepreneurs.

PART ONE

CHAPTER ONE

Having A Global Mindset: Seeing Yourself Beyond The Country And City You Live In

DO YOU HAVE TO travel to develop a global mindset? Not really, a global perspective is an inner interest that someone sets to learn about various cultural backgrounds. A global mindset is the capability to adapt, recognize, and read other cultural symbols. As a result, your efficiency is not affected when interacting with different communities. In our daily life, the aptitude to study and process information for everyday judgments gets restricted. Our brains find a way to correct it by filtering the surge of information streaming from the outside world. As time progresses, the filtering becomes a permanent character that determines an individual's response to a situation. This personality trait defines a person's mindset.

The global mindset has its impact on the business world too. Its significance in companies is based on the research done by Bartlett and Ghoshal. They agreed that international companies should focus on networked executives to prosper. This is mainly because people from various cultures respond differently to training and presentations. In a multicultural organization, it is almost impossible to perform without a global mindset. Based on CultureWizard analysis, practically 1400 companies that embraced a global mindset performed much better. A global mindset is not the only basis in any intercontinental interactions. Companies that aspire to spread their wings into the international market should embrace it. Fortunately, it is a learnable skill to get and easy to measure too.

How to Measure Global Mindset

The rising density of intercultural jobs and inadequate guidance has resulted in headship challenges in companies. There is scarce literature in the market that guides on how to penetrate the multiracial market. A group of professors known as the Thunderbird group analyzed the topic. They researched how to categorize the main attributes and qualities for global market success. They examined 23 cities in the United States, Asia, and Europe and spoke to more than 5,000 executives. In a great length, they touched on successes and failures that executives face while interacting with other cultures. The study also reflected on how executives understand a global mindset leadership's effectiveness in a cross-culture environment.

One of the team members, Professor Mansour Javidan, explained further. He mentioned that different people have various ways of defining and solving a problem. Thus, solutions to a similar issue may vary depending on a person's background. A leader in such an organization should strive to create a consensus for people who bring different opinions to the table. With increased globalization, most employers will work with people from different cultures. Javidan clarifies that people experience challenges working with other cultures based on how they grew up. He says, "The problem is that children grow up mostly learning how to live and work with people who are like them. So when a corporation requests the managerial to effectively work with people from other parts of the world, it's asking managers to do something different from what they know." Organizations are expected to empower their executives on the new global expectations. That's the real meaning of a global mindset.

Compared to a low global mindset, a high one brings along motivation and not intimidation. Such individuals understand how politics, economics, and culture systems work in other countries. Thus, they are empowered to create trusting relationships with people from various cultures. They manage that by practicing active listening and showing empathy and respect. The thunder team came up with a building tool to measure a global mindset. It is referred to as the Global Mindset Inventory (GMI). Each person's global mindset is measured on three main dimensions and nine secondary ones. Below are the three primary dimensions.

Global Psychological Capital

This is the most significant characteristic of the global mindset. It concentrates on the manager's expressive energy and the willingness to use it in the worldwide environment. It also denotes an optimistic and constructive attitude towards the diversification of actions and thoughts.

Global Social Capital

This is the behavior feature of the global mindset. It refers to the executive's ability to help create a trusting affiliation with employees from different corners of the world. Social capital is based on the human capacity to consider others and act generously. It mainly focuses on relations in an organization that bear prolific benefits.

Global Intellectual Capital

This is the cognitive facet of the global mindset. It refers to what the management understands as the international aspect of the industry. It touches on the more expansive macro atmosphere's knowledge and how the executive can scrutinize, digest, and infer the information.

The nine secondary mindsets are sub dived beneath the primary ones. Under the psychological capital, there are; passion for diversity, the quest for adventure, and self-assurance. Global social capital covers, intercultural empathy, interpersonal impact, and diplomacy. Finally, global intellectual capital entails cognitive complexity, cosmopolitan outlook, and international business savvy. All dimensions are interrelated for more efficiency. For instance, global psychological capital assists the management in influencing their worldwide intellectual to the subordinates.

In some cases, an executive may have a vast knowledge of other cultures but is biased to work with people that come from those places. The psychological capital comes in place to balance the equation. If introduced in an organization, it empowers the management to empower the team on the importance of a global mindset.

How to Introduce Global Mindset in an Organization?

Various organizations globalize at different rates and ways based on strategic options and locality. Companies that embrace globalization at a higher speed find a need to adopt a global mindset. Whatever the route a firm may choose, there are basic requirements for effectual adaption. From the start, employees should get empowerment to start thinking from a global perspective. For instance, in an organization that designs products for the local market, the employees need to have a global need in mind. They should receive enlightenment on complications that arise from operating business on an international scale. The global market requires an extensive understanding of everyday collaboration between the employees and business units. Regardless of its locality, it should share the purpose of worldwide efficiency and convey vital international knowledge.

Introducing a global mindset allows the staff in the headquarters to consult with others worldwide. This enables the organization to cultivate expertise and knowledge based on other key markets worldwide. Every employee should be empowered to address various issues happening in any branch worldwide. This helps in creating an innovative approach to solutions and an overhaul generated balance. In most organizations, it is tempting to go for quick fixes in cultural challenges. In a real sense, such approaches do not work for a long time. Instead, cultural awareness is a skill that's acquired gradually and requires patience. Adopting a multi-faceted approach is beneficial in attaining positive results and creating momentum. Here are basic guidelines to adapt to the system.

Premeditated Planning

Any organization should take into account the intensity of growth, investment, and hiring. This should be based on local and international markets. When management does not have a clear picture of the international markets, progress gets affected. This may land it into losses due to over-investing or under-investing. Strategic options like pricing, branding, and product development must be driven from a global perspective. This approach incorporates the aspirations and needs of the consumers in the market for a positive outcome.

Introduce Multi-Media Communication

In a familiar running organization, employees can get used to the old way of operating. Sometimes they get skeptical about fresh innovations. But if some new global information can tinkle in, it can change the whole dimension. Currently, various media platforms support employees in adapting to global roles. Some of them include virtual meetings, online video clips, e-learning platforms, and webinars. The list also is interactive language learning avenues and web tools. These tools offer data about local and international business customs. Organizations should experiment with fresh approaches to encourage a global mindset.

Leadership Learning and Improvement on Global Mindset

Cultural based programs are beneficial, especially when integrated with global perspectives. Employees gain a lot from such sessions, which can be achieved in several ways. Some of them are video conferencing, direct engagement, or advanced interviews. Training coaches should incorporate international insights and objectives. Best performing companies take their executives to crucial performing countries. They intend to give them a firsthand experience on how to reinforce international aspects. Organizations that incorporate international assignments experience rapid cost-cutting and progress. All companies should create a close connection with a network of people all over the world. These people should appreciate, trust, and guide each other on their cultural approaches. When employees get exposed to different markets, they understand the importance of information. Expatriates are strong holders of these values. Thanks to the vast exposure in other locations. Temporary assignments mostly hosted in luxury hotels are a reasonable basis too. But the impact is more forceful when someone interrelates with different culture for a longer time. There is a vast difference between visiting and living in an area. Even if it's for a couple of months, living has a more express and unfiltered experience.

5 POINTS I HAVE LEARNED IN MY JOURNEY TO GOING GLOBAL

1 ____

2 ____

3 ____

4 ____

5 ____

CHAPTER 2

Develop Your Brand And Tap Into Far Reaching Platforms

"Go ye therefore, and teach all nations, baptizing them in the name of the Father, and of the Son, and of the Holy Ghost." (Mathew 20:19 KJV).

JESUS CHRIST ADMONISHED US to preach the Gospel to the world, churches and ministries need to spread the Gospel of our Lord and Saviour Jesus Christ through the greatest worldwide communication tool which is the Internet. In the days of the Bible, there was no social media, websites, or even internet, yet the message of the Gospel reached the whole world. Now that we have a platform that brings the world together, you need to leverage it to develop your brand and advance the Kingdom of God. With the help of social media, you can engage an audience wider than you can even locate, farther than your imagination, and deeper than your knowledge.

Branding is the perception of people about you or your business. Your personal brand is the uniqueness that distinguishes you from others. It covers your values, skills, talents, and knowledge. Your personal brand can be packaged and projected via a platform that may be on the pulpit, organizational meetings, conferences, social media, websites, or podcasts.

Developing a consistent brand can help people recognize your projected identity and message. Jesus provided a personal touch. He was visible and spoke to the people in a language that they understood through stories and parables. His brand personality stood out. He related with everyone both young and old.

While you develop your brand, take your message to platforms where people are rather than expecting them to come to you or your websites. It takes value, packaging, and proper projection to engage the online community, and convert casual audience or readers to consistent readers and ardent followers.

Social media platforms such as Facebook and Instagram are very popular, and so are *sites that allow people to broadcast messages, such as YouTube and Twitter. There are also online conferencing applications such as Zoom and Free Conference App. You must do a good research on the right platform you want to use to get, engage, and manage your audience.

While you build your brand, you must be able to balance your real identity and your projected personality. What you project yourself as must be consistent with who you are in Christ. Then, you must really work on your motive. The challenge of digital platforms is the tendency to project us than it does to our message. But when we are sure that our focus is to get value and our message reaching out to lives to the glory of God, our hearts can be secured in God.

Then you need to know the exact thing you want to do online. This will influence the activities, structure, operations, and functions of your ministry or business that will be digitally inclined. You need to build a team of people who understand your vision, values, and identity to keep them on the track of followers or audience engagement. Responsibility should be given to trained individuals who know what to do and how to get things done.

Create a structure to work it. Everything that works have a structure that makes it works. A structure gives guidelines to the plans, activities, and contents that will be used to engage the audience. You need to also create brand rules that will engage your organizational or personal beliefs and core values.

Set markers and goals to help you monitor your strategy. You will need to monitor your search engine rankings, the contents that engage people more, and the increase in followership. While the motive is not the number, we also need to remember that the number of believers added to the church was monitored and recorded for us to read. So, we must ensure that the objectives of the platforms are being met, and the people are getting blessed by the content we place on those platforms. For businesses, we must monitor the call to action and the effectiveness of the digital strategy we employ.

Also, to develop your brand, you must be a though leader in your niche. You must develop brand integrity that people can trust with infallible resources. You must be willing to study the culture of people in your field and dare to be different by being relevant and also by going counter-culture.

Finally, having an audience is not the same as engaging them. You can make your platforms more engaging by making your activities audience-oriented. Let them have the power to decide to an extent what happens on the platform to encourage engagement.

5 POINTS I HAVE LEARNED IN MY JOURNEY TO GOING GLOBAL

1 ______________________________

____

2 ______________________________

____

3 ______________________________

____

4 ______________________________

____

5 ______________________________

____

CHAPTER 3

Leading And Not Managing

EVERY CHRISTIAN IS BORN to lead in one or more spheres of life. Leadership in God's Kingdom is not by status, position, or degree, but a responsibility we must take up because everything rests on leadership. God created us to fulfill a specific purpose, and this assignment is to be achieved with God's gifts, wisdom, and potentials in us and this in turn influences your area or field of leadership.

One of the challenges of leaders is the confusion of leadership and management. The inability to differentiate between these has turned leaders into managers. Although the two terms are important and are often used interchangeably, they are very much different. As Christians, we are not called to manage, but to lead. We are not called to manage the lives under our care, but to provide Godly leadership that is inspired by purpose and achieved by influence.

The issue with many people is that they are taught to manage and not lead, and this has led to many churches being managed, and not being led. Management has even led Christian gatherings to do activities rather than influencing the system. Management is not all bad but must be balanced with effective leadership. Management creates a sense of being a master, while leadership creates a sense of being a servant.

Jesus Christ addressed the mentality among the disciples when they had arguments about who will be their leader. While they argue, Jesus could see the intent of their hearts and could understand their perspectives and beliefs about leadership. The Bible says,

> **"And Jesus calling them to Him and said, you know that the rulers of the Gentiles lord it over them, and their great men hold them in subjection [tyrannizing over them]. Not so shall it be among you; but whoever wishes to be great among you must be your servant, and whoever desires to be first among you must be your slave – just as the Son of Man came not to be waited on but to serve, and to give His life as a ransom for many [the price paid to set them free]." (Mathew 20:25-28 AMP).**

The disciples grew up with a leadership mentality they saw among the gentiles, and they had seen how the rulers lord it over their followers, and made them subjects to them. Jesus told them,

> "It shall not be so among you." (Mathew 20:26 ESV).

This simply means that leadership in the secular context is not the same as leadership in God's Kingdom. The things obtainable in secular leadership are not in Christianity. I love the way the Message Bible explains the scenario:

> "...So Jesus got them together to settle things down. He said, "You've observed how godless rulers throw their weight around, how quickly a little power goes to their heads. It's not going to be that way with you. Whoever wants to be great must become a servant. Whoever wants to be first among you must be your slave. That is what the Son of Man has done: He came to serve, not to be served – and then give away his life in exchange for the many who are held hostage." (Mathew 20:25-28 MSG).

We can manage resources, but not people. We are to lead as examples in all ramifications of our lives, living a life that is worthy of emulation. The difference between leading and managing is vision. Leadership is driven by vision. While managing involves analyzing and planning to solve problems, leadership rests on the vision and character of the leader. We are called to lead by vision, not manage by analyzing.

We must focus more on leading than managing. We must provide leadership with excellence. A leader says 'we', manager says 'I'. The focus of leadership is on the growth and improvement of the followers, while management focuses on outcome. Beyond communicating vision, value, and God kind of life, we are to embody the vision, value, and God kind of life, in such a way that we can be correct sons and daughters like our Father.

Leadership is by influence and emulation, not mere communication. Our lives should be more eloquent to communicate the goodness of God than our lips. The body of Christ has so dwelled on evangelism by speaking, than by living. If we live by all we speak, we will influence our world more. You are called to lead, and leadership lies in what you do than what you say. Your life is the first testament to leadership. If you can lead your life well, then you will become a global figure. Many people in the world today cannot even lead their lives, not to talk about leading others. If you can rise to the responsibility of leading, and not just managing, you can become an influencer for the Kingdom.

Leaders are responsible for the welfare of the people led. This can be quite difficult if we are managing and not leading. When we manage, we often do not bother about the welfare of the people but instead our expectations from them. In the end, the expectations may be met, but the people will not become any better. When the interest of those we lead is in our heart, we are not only concerned about the outcomes, but also their development and welfare. The goal of leadership is not only to achieve but to ultimately develop more leaders who can achieve.

Leadership by Vision

> "Where there is no vision, the people perish: but he that keepeth the law, happy is he." (Proverbs 29:18 KJV).

Lack of vision makes people perish. When there is a vision, people grow better. When there is a vision, people know what goals to reach forth to. Vision brings people together in unity. Vision removes the tendency to manipulate people and commits leaders to lead and not manage them.

As leaders, you should be able to plan and structure an achievable future. Vision is a picture of the future that is sourced and informed by the scriptures and inspired by God. There is a vision when we realize our assignment in whatever capacity we are called to serve. There is a vision when we know what God wants to achieve in and through us. Vision speaks of the destination. God speaks in visions because He sees the end from the beginning.

In the Bible, we see leaders who receive vision and instructions, and they were executed effectively. Noah was given the vision to save lives and was instructed to build an ark (Genesis 6). Visions have the potentials to save the lives of people. David went to the Cave of Adullam, and about four hundred men came to him (1 Samuel 22). He became their leader and captain, and in the end, these men became mighty men of David. Leadership builds men to become better versions of who they are. When there is a vision, people get better. When leaders build others, they end up being built into better and more effective leaders.

Leaders should receive and live by vision. Vision creates responsibility for its fulfillment. It is not just a statement or information but it carries a sense of purpose, urgency, and passion. Vision is an alignment with the revelation of God for a people. The Bible says,

> **"Where there is no revelation, people cast off restraint; but blessed is the one who heeds wisdom's instruction." (Proverbs 29:18 NIV).**

The fact that we lead humans suggests that there will be a tendency for people to cast off restraint and live outside the will of God, but vision serves as a hedge to protect them within the confines of wisdom and instructions. Vision shapes people and cuts excesses. Whatever your assignment may be in your organization, church, or ministry, your responsibility is to clarify, communicate, and ultimately live by vision.

Vision creates responsibility for leadership. As leaders, knowing that we are examples to those we lead commits us to develop ourselves, potentials, gifts, skills, and careers. It is possible that you so much focus on the development of others that you forget the need to develop yourself. You must also have a leader whom you can look up to as others look up to you. Leaders communicate the need for development with their personal and professional development.

Leadership by Action

> **"In my former book, Theophilus, I wrote about all that Jesus began to do and to teach." (Acts 1:1 NIV).**

Jesus lived an exemplary life that was worthy of emulation, and we saw the impact of this on the disciples. They did not just do what Jesus did; they became conformed to His image. As we lead, we must be conscious of the need for representation, and not just a representative of Christ. We must embody Christ, and make Him exalted in all we do. Jesus did not teach and do but did and taught. He taught them through His actions than He did through His words. In leadership, actions are more profound than words.

Leadership is acting, not talking. A manager says "go," but a leader says "let us go." Apostle Paul while demonstrating leadership told the people of Corinthians,

> **"Follow my example, as I follow the example of Christ." (1 Corinthians 11:1 NIV).**

He encouraged people to follow his example. It takes leadership to serve as a good and Godly example for others. A Christian leader must be one whose life portrays the life of Christ. Do not follow a man who is not following Christ. You can learn from people, but we are called to follow Christ. It takes a good follower to be a good leader. Paul the Apostle was a committed follower of Christ, and this made him a good leader. We are to lead an exemplary life that is worth emulating at work, home, in the church, and in the neighborhood.

A Christian leader must understand that his social media platforms are not just merely inclined socially, but instruments to reach forth to a wider audience. Every post, reaction, and picture speaks much about you. Your words matter to the people. When people visit your profile on social media or blogs, they want to learn and get inspired by your words, actions, and inactions about the matters of life. As much as our personal representation matters, we need to know that our social representation matters in this twenty-first century.

5 POINTS I HAVE LEARNED IN MY JOURNEY TO GOING GLOBAL

1 ____________________

____

2 ____________________

____

3 ____________________

____

4 ____________________

____

5 ____________________

____

CHAPTER 4

Being Created To Lead And Express Your Gifts And Greatness To The World

SOMETIMES YOU MAY WONDER if you have a unique attribute. I am sure you are not alone in this. But have you ever thought about those things that keep you focused? Maybe you have a passion for cooking, painting, or even dancing? Or probably you frequently get elected into leading positions but have never connected it with talents? In some cases, people associate such with fate. In reality, it is not; God is behind it all. He does not give us these special skills for fame or money. He desires us to honor him and bless others through them. 1 Peter 4:10 says, "Each of you should use whatever gift you have received to serve others as faithful stewards of God's grace in its various forms." Peter is talking about the spiritual gifts of healing and prophecies. They are the mystical capabilities given to the followers of Christ. When he mentions blessing others, it falls over to our talents. God did not give them to us for our benefit but to others too. However, some people would love to help but feel like they have nothing to offer. In short, they have not realized the special skills deposited in them yet.

For God put each one of us in the world with a set of unique talents. Romans 12:6 says, *"Since we have gifts that differ according to the grace given to us, each of us is to exercise them accordingly: if prophecy, according to the portion of his faith."* God's words here are a clear reminder that we all possess a distinctive gift from one another. He has a specific purpose of planting those gifts into us. In the same way, you have a mission of seeking and finding them. Through the journey of life, you may find yourself drawn to something. That is the first signal of identifying your talents. Still, some people might struggle to pinpoint them. Sometimes it is not about the level of brilliance in finding them; it requires God's guidance. Invite Him to unveil them and empower you on how to implement them. Below are three genuine ways of discovering your talents.

Track Down Your Passion Journey

What did you love doing as a child? To most people, this is the basis of their talents. List down the activities that helped you in the past days. Maybe you killed your boredom by knitting or assisting in the kitchen. Check if these activities gave you excitement and satisfaction. Ask yourself if you progressed with them while growing up. If something lights up and keeps you motivated, then you must be good at it. Human beings love to associate with things that do not strain them. If you do not struggle with that blueberry cake, then your talent lies in the kitchen.

Discover the Significant Thing in Your Life

Various areas of life encase a human being. They might vary but mostly include family, career, health, and religion. Some people also embrace relationships, recreation, and personal growth. Among all these values, you should categorize those that you hold on to firmly. Through them, you may realize how you value life. They also come as a guide on what you want to achieve. If your main priority is family, you should focus on creating a functional one. When you identify your favorite values, you can connect them with purpose and passion. For instance, you can use your culinary skills to give your family satisfaction.

Inquire From Others

If you are still struggling to find your talent, ask those close to you.

I am sure you have a few persons that you spend time with. It can be a colleague or a family member. Those are the people who understand you better. By spending time together, they have seen your true colors. They can easily spot that unique attribute that you possess.

How to Use Your Gifts in Leadership?

Once you've acknowledged your talents, you can comfortably move on to implementing them. It would help if you explored the ways that surround them. Note that you do not have to be a pro in those areas. What matters is the comfort they give to you and others. Remember that what you give is unique and sacred. Whatever you are offering makes a big difference in the world. God wants us to use our unique gifts to create an impact. Leadership is one way of influencing the communities we live in. The Holy Spirit guides God's given headship. Romans 12: 8 says, *"If it is to encourage, then encourage; if it is giving, then give generously; if it to lead, do it diligently; if it is to show mercy, do it cheerfully."* He wants us to use the leadership gift to protect, assist, and care for others. From this verse, leadership is slotted between the gifts of mercy and giving, on purpose. God wants us to understand its significance in caring for others.

Caring is typically connected to charity or money giving. But in leadership, it holds more content beyond any value. It involves giving people chances, benefits of doubts, and a reason to want the association with you. These values allow you to give others a leeway to make mistakes while learning. They also empower you to guide others on the job. By giving them the authority to make decisions, they acquire responsibility. Credible leadership is all about giving credit to others. It translates to the generosity of the Holy Spirit. Generosity is a dignified aspect of leadership. Decades ago, in English speaking countries, generosity was associated with nobility. The privileged were expected to help the needy. Leadership in current days should also portray the same virtues. A leader should show the way that's generously guided by a clear mind. He should delegate duties that empower. With such kind of exposure, a seed of growth and development is planted. Thus, becomes a motivation for those working under you. Such workers give unobstructed efforts in their roles. Here are five ways that a leader should use their gifts to lead others.

Ways to lead

Empower People with Your Knowledge

A realistic leader's main plan is to give power to his people. Through expertise and good practice, they can enrich their lives. As mentioned in the Mindtools blog, a leader known as James Welch spent hours teaching numerous executives. Discussed also is Andy Grove, former Intel CEO. This man devoted his whole time to train staff on the philosophy of leading. He taught them how to remain relevant in an industry where innovations get outdated real fast. From their vast knowledge, these men made positive strides in their positions.

Be a Light to Others

This is an extraordinary aspect that helps others to grow and shine. There is so much satisfaction when your boss embraces the open door policy. When a leader is involved in your roles, you feel more valued. It motivates even more when your presence is acknowledged. Such kind of leadership also comes with an outstanding level of integrity. It refers to being trustworthy, reliable, and honest. Leaders who possess integrity practice what they preach. They follow their words to the letter and own up to their mistakes. When you lead people with such values, they will always respect and want to associate with you. In the long run, they will introduce those values on their own,

Give others Chances

Another valuable aspect of leadership is giving opportunities to those under you. We have so many people in society who lack confidence. Such people require a leader who holds their hands and not reprimands. Probably, life has already given them enough beating. It would help if you strived to offer a shoulder to lean on. Through your talents, find a way to embrace them. If you are good at playing the guitar, you can introduce a happy hour of music on Fridays. Music is always therapeutic and comforting. From these sessions, that timid colleague can eventually get out of the shell.

Practice Forgiveness

Martin Luther King Jnr once said that the law of an eye to an eye call leave everyone blind. There is both humor and truth in that statement. But what he meant was that when you hold onto bitterness, you punish yourself more. A generous leader holds no resentment. The Bible talks about that in different verses. For instance, Colossians 3:13 says, *"Bearing with one another and, if one has a complaint against one another, forgiving each other as the Lord has forgiven you, so you also must forgive."* A leader should practice those words accordingly. No one is perfect, but there are better ways to solve a conflict.

Motivate and not Criticize

If you are the type of leader that pulls others down, you have no focus. Possibly, your employee turnover must be on the higher side. There is that moment that your employee will not meet goals. Maybe that report was not formatted to your liking. You do not have to shout and let everyone know about your disappointment. Instead, you can guide them on it. Sometimes it is not through ignorance that people fail. They are probably not aware of what to do. Through your expertise, you can save a whole lot of scenarios.

5 POINTS I HAVE LEARNED IN MY JOURNEY TO GOING GLOBAL

1 ______________________________

2 ______________________________

3 ______________________________

4 ______________________________

5 ______________________________

CHAPTER 5

What Is Vision Statement?

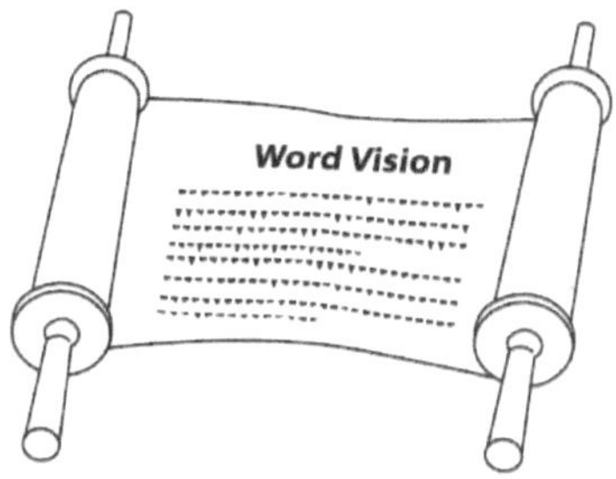

VISION STATEMENTS EXPRESS THE future objectives of an organization or any entity. Writing a powerful statement is an overwhelming task. Not only is it supposed to delineate the present and future goals, but it should create an impact too. Once you have one running, it guides the distribution of funds and decisions. For instance, Disney's vision statement says, "To make people happy." It shows how one summarizes focus and provides guidance on how to achieve a goal. Katie Taylor, CEO of Untold Content, adds by saying, "It serves a superior purpose to harness all the company's foresight into one impactful statement." More research documented in the Business News Daily confirms that the engagement levels of an employee are high in companies with a strong vision statement. Up to 68% of them are more productive and active ambassadors. In short, it forms a reliable way for employees and stakeholders to comprehend their purpose in the company's success. With such a significant impact on the company's achievements, it is effective to create a statement that combines goals and motivates the staff.

How to Develop a Vision Statement?

The initial step in crafting one is concluding on whom to do it. It is easier to do it in smaller businesses by compiling the insights of all employees. But in large corporations, it requires a selection of representatives. Brandon Shockley, a Branding & Marketing Research Director, suggested a sequence of representative workshops to create alternate statement versions. The rest of the organization should give feedback before concluding on the best. There is no definite outline of writing one, but some successful brands have included the following traits.

Short and Clear

A vision statement is not an avenue to write so much. Instead, it should be straightforward and readable. The main focus is to hit the market and create a positive impact successfully.

Despite its shortness, it should convince the audience of the company's capabilities.

Inspire the Staff

While setting your goals, you should not hesitate to get out of the box. Strive to create objectives that are not too simple to achieve but not impractical and demeaning.

Focus on the Future

This is merely a fixed duration in the future to achieve your goals. You need to assess the vision statement and identify the exact time. Remember that its purpose is on future accomplishments and not the present.

Create an all balanced Statement

A positive statement should be firm in the market and not swayed but technological innovations. It should also display the company's strategic plans and interests.

Mission Statement

A mission statement briefly communicates the purpose within the organization and in public. It does not clarify profitable operations but defines the motivation behind the returns. The main difference between mission and vision statements is that the former concentrates on the present during the later on the future. Most mission statements progress and change over the years. While it's ideal for crafting them from the beginning, it requires consistent analysis to define the company's current principles. Each successful company should have one as a basis for efficient planning. Since they are also associated with an organization's public opinion, they are often used for marketing purposes. Some are portrayed in the intro part of the website and become the hub of the company's campaigns. A well-defined one should lead to tactical focus and motivates the employees to work as a team.

How to Develop Mission Statements?

For any business, daily operations sometimes get in the way. A perfect mission statement comes in handy to refresh and keep you on toes about its core purposes. Here are five ideas on how to develop an ideal mission statement.

Start by Defining the Market

You are not required to write a story but to reflect on it as a guideline. A defining story clarifies the uniqueness of your company and the target market. If you are having trouble getting started, list the do's and don'ts of the company first.

Define Your Business Operations to the Customers

To create a positive impact, you need to portray your strengths. Using the market-defining story, you can reach out to your target market. Make sure not to underestimate your organization. Instead, create a factual statement to define what your business does and the solutions to offer.

Describe Your operations to the Employees

For any successful company, keeping the staff happy is the foundation for a good turnover. Rewarding and appreciating keeps them focused on the objectives. You can do that by mentioning room for growth, fair salaries, and a healthy working environment. Even if the company has not perfected the mentioned aspects, they can serve as mementos for future aspirations.

Identify The Company Connection with the Owners

In the real sense, a company exists to improve the finances of the owners. Thus, a strong mission statement should incorporate the proprietor's strengths merged with others to achieve the company's objectives.

Be Open-minded

Mission statements define various functions and objectives; caution is required when creating one. Combine all the required information for internal and public use. Several companies have segmented statements to categorize the goals. It would help if you strived to do all work. If required, review and revise them as your company grows.

Personal Branding

It is a continuing practice of evolving and maintaining status as an impression to a particular group, organization, or individual. While some carry-outs concentrate on self-upgrading, personal branding identifies triumph as self-packaging. It is more about how you promote yourself with a distinctive blend of experience, personality, and skills for your followers to view and emulate. There are various guidelines on ideal personal branding. Here are three of the most popular ones.

Get Purposeful

Several flourishing marketers define their success through consistent creation and sharing of content. The strategy does not always work mainly because of one thing; lack of intention. Setting up a budget and plan can endorse the content availability rather than create new ones each time. It is vital also to depict content that the market wants to see and not what you assume. Strive to identify your target market and give them what they want.

Practice Consistency

Ensure that your digital channels are constant by representing the dominant person you aspire. You can go out of your way to offer free and valuable information to the people. Try to stick to one niche to avoid confusing your followers on different topics.

Discover a Unique Promotion Proposition

To maximize personal branding, you need to recognize your brand's distinctiveness to stand out above the rest. A brand that has benefitted a lot from personal branding is Coca-Cola. They succeed by associating the drink with the kind of lifestyle people would love to lead.

Corporate Branding

This broad term swathes around marketing concerns of an organization and their interrelationship with each other. It is the foundation of a business that portrays itself to the world and the employees as well. For a new business, you need to focus on a precise direction. The brand reflection is a continuous effort of the partners, staff, customers, and other stakeholders. Each of them has a specific role directly or indirectly. Most thriving organizations use slogans, symbols, and logos that symbolize their services and products. Sometimes, they come in the form of traditions, distinctiveness, and promises. It is not easy to come up with a great corporate brand. Most individuals complain of a lack of time, resources, or energy to start over. Here are some simplified ways;

Ways to Develop a Corporate Brand...

Execute a Brand Review

To fix any problem, you need to figure out the problem first. An audit of the current brand is the starting step. Concentrate on the visual, messaging, website, printing, and others. Calculate the strengths and weaknesses and figure out what needs to go. Do not forget to assess also what the competitor is putting on the table.

Involve everyone to Establish your Brand's Purpose

Get representatives from all departments and discuss the principle of the company. Also, put across a dialogue about products, services, reviews, missions, and so forth. Get someone to head the meeting or hire an outsourced expert. From there, involve the rest of the company. Give questionnaires to the staff to get feedback on the changes they would want in the company. This helps the organization team to get on the same page with the subordinates.

Breathe Life in your Brand

With all the information available now, it is time to create a fused brand strategy. You need to embody it visually with a logo. For an emblem that will last a lifetime, engage a credible designer with huge references.

Build up Guidelines

A reliable brand should have colors, fonts, and images that represent the company. The staff should be empowered to understand the brand rules and follow them. If the rules are not adequately implemented, consistency will get thrown out of the window. As a result, your brand will be a thing of failure.

5 POINTS I HAVE LEARNED IN MY JOURNEY TO GOING GLOBAL

1 ____

2 ____

3 ____

4 ____

5 ____

CHAPTER 6

What Is Team Building?

TEAM BUILDING IS BONDS intensification amongst members to increase efficiency and achieving goals. Through a course of action, members share values and universal expectations. The team building structure is guided by a set of norms that aids members to interact better. Sometimes, it involves planned activities led by squad leaders or external resources. For instance, it can start with a picnic in a nearby park. Members can grill food and pass around. Such an activity intends to assemble, create quality time and bond over the meal. If the workers take the food and eat alone in their offices, it beats team building's logic. Group activities like hiking, bowling, and ball games contribute a lot to the bonding. Some demanding physical activities like rock climbing cause fear for inactive members. Try to abstain from them and stick to what the staff can take part in comfortably.

The main activities should be cheap, practical, and fun. You can get innovative and come up with amusing activities that will not cost the company much. Using a hired expert also helps in coercing teamwork spirit by the use of organized activities. Teamwork is more efficient when activities get customized to the group's needs. Despite team building creating a positive impact, it is not comparable to a customized event. These episodes are icebreakers in brainstorming, discussing key topics, and cooperative coursework. The key is for the facilitator to lead the team to achieve its goals by integrating different activities every day.

Importance of Team Building

Team building is essential to an enjoyable and trustworthy working environment. Creating a reliable team does not happen by hiring kind and proficient people alone. The basis is helping them recognize diversification and its importance while working together. A team leader should focus on hosting one of two team building activities annually. Below are ten reasons why you should introduce team building in an organization:

Helps Resolve Variances

Disagreements are prone to happen in any organization due to different opinions. It is up to the members to solve them cordially and not blow out into disputes. Conflicts in a working environment are not always a negative occurrence. Sometimes, they can result in constructive work if solved well. If people with diverse interests get grouped, their principles add value to an organization. Solving such issues is encouraged by allowing openness among individuals. By appreciating different perspectives, members learn to appreciate others and achieve more.

Introducing Healthy Competition

Team building activities bring out the competitive perspective of each employee. It is verified that if you introduce a competitive task, members attain more. Team building activities are mostly fun games where participants compete to complete challenges. These actions' primary purpose is to cultivate team spirit and acquire other skills like communication and amicable problem-solving.

Strengthen Trust amongst Workers

In any effective team, trust is vital. For teams to work together, they need to be able to rely on one another if the need arises. Besides, when reliance is nurtured among members, it allows them to give each other space to make decisions and complete tasks. Trusts keep people at ease and help them to open up. Through this, members discuss their weaknesses and strengths. As a result, they are more proactive in taking risks, giving ideas, and arriving at a consensus. In the end, the company experiences improved communication. The enhanced collaboration also assists members in exposing each other vulnerability and work better as a team.

Enhance Productivity

Teamwork involves the sharing of workloads within an organization. In short, one member with fewer assignments can assist another to complete their job. When roles get shared, workload finishes faster, improving the overall productivity of an organization. Teamwork also improves individual productivity. Due to individuals working as a team, they learn new skills from one another—this perk ups overall team performance by efficient running and working more in less time. At the end, companies generate more returns while achieving their targets.

Standardize Communication

As mentioned above, teamwork even out communication in an organization. When team members converse about the task at hand, they achieve better results. Communication aids them to plan and do the assignment most efficiently. It also allows staff to appreciate their role in an organization and the importance of other colleagues. When team members understand the different functions, they help each other out in achieving goals. In an environment where employees are free to air out their views, impressive results are noticed.

Allow People to Accept Each Other

This is one of the most important benefits of team working. Working places are becoming broader towards gender and cultural diversity. In any organization, everyone should receive similar significance and resources to achieve goals. It is ideal for forming teams with individuals from varied ethnic backgrounds. This empowers them to appreciate and understand each other dissimilarities. It also helps staff to keep from biased judgments that break the purpose of working as a team. Improving interpersonal relationships in workplaces helps staff to share both victories and failures. Each of them brings forth varied opinions in tackling issues within the organization. At the end, it brings them closer and builds on reliance. When one member helps one another, the other will return the favor later.

Improve the Organization's Culture

Working together fosters innovation and creativity in the workplace. When employees collaborate and communicate more, they improve their efficiency and performance. Through collaboration, conflicts get resolved cordially, resulting in individuals appreciating each other more. Through appreciation, more people get recognized and it motivates them to achieve more. This improves the company's performance and fosters an optimistic, motivating working environment.

Promote Inspiration and Learning

When different people work together and get along, innovative thoughts from bottom to the top, organizations with an open door policy allow members to interact freely and promote innovations. Compared to working solo, team working creates room for new perspectives and ideas. It integrates personal experiences with others to make work more efficient and fun. In the end, all team members are comfortable bringing something new to the table and gain knowledge from each other.

Creating Happier Teams

When you walk into a store, and you get welcomed with beaming faces, happiness is shared by anyone around. For an organization to reach that level, there is a lot of teamwork done behind the scenes. A contented team is excited to work in an organization and more likely to stay there for a long time. When they blissfully work with each other, they give clients better service. As a result, you develop loyal customers who refer others to fulfilling returns.

Fosters Leadership and Accountability Skills

Working as a team involves some staff taking on leadership responsibilities to overlook others. For a team to execute duties and achieve goals, it must come to a consensus before making decisions. It requires members to communicate and listen to one another actively. These discussions empower them in decision making, strategies, and solving issues. It also helps them to get accountable for their actions and decisions.

Factors Affecting Team Building

Despite the success brought about by team building, it requires consistency to assemble a productive team. To create a prolific team, you need to understand common factors that affect this joint effort and solve them. Here are tips to guide you through:

Concentrate on the Goals

A typical goal guides team success. To maximize this, the goals should be spelled out in advance, and members made to understand them. Team success is achieved by giving priority to the group's goals. The objectives should be in writing for everyone to see, comprehend, and work through attaining them. The members should strive for a deeper understanding of the goals for more effortless accomplishment.

Insist on Solid Communication

Communication in an organization is on two levels; between employees and from the executive to the team. For team success, there should be an all-round open communication. It should be cultivated even out of the office to enhance relationships. The executive should offer training and update the team regularly on any new developments for smooth running.

Encourage Affirmative Approach

For effective teams, members should have positive attitudes towards the company, project, and one another. If team members are not conversant with one another, you can introduce casual meetings. These meetings encourage members to share experiences, generate bonds, and create trust. For easy sharing, strive to have offices nearer to each other. Please keep track of negative people, support them to change or do away with them.

Eliminate Compensation Hindrances

Teamwork is enhanced when members receive compensation for their efforts. Before assembling a team, it is ideal to come up with an effective compensation plan. If payment issues are laid down before signing the contract, they eliminate this obstacle. Also, if the team receives additional payments, they perform much better.

Handle Conflicts

As documented in the Chron blog, conflicts should be dealt with as soon as they arise. If not, they discourage the team from achieving its objectives. To create a reliable team, an organization should introduce measures of controlling conflicts to improve performance.

5 POINTS I HAVE LEARNED IN MY JOURNEY TO GOING GLOBAL

1 ____

2 ____

3 ____

4 ____

5 ____

CHAPTER 7

Creating Value

HAVE YOU FELT LIKE your life is at a standstill? Sometimes life gives a cold shoulder, and things fall apart. It may get to a point that every effort you make falls flat on your face. As you grind harder, it gets worse even when you give it your best. It is more depressing when you witness progress in other people's lives. Probably, they are relatives or close friends. They do not struggle as you do, yet their lives are thriving. Everything they touch flourishes and gets better each passing day. Before making some weird judgments about your predicaments, get the facts right. Apparently, your friends are approaching life from a different perspective. There is a universal belief of' we reap what we sow' that most successful people use. Most likely, this is the principle you have failed to incorporate in your weak spots. Like it or not, but this principle is the basis of a successful. Some people may link their misfortunes to karma or even curses.

The truth is that they are getting it all wrong. The value that life gives us is significant to the one we create. We do not get it any other way. The secret is to start the value creation journey soonest. We should embrace it in the passage of life. By engaging with others positively, we strengthen the pedestal. Value is also created by seeking opportunities to assist others. To approach things soberly, you need to involve your body, mind and soul. Get out of the box and augment the quality of your life. You can start simply with an appearance change. Dye your hair to a new color or even change your wardrobe. Do not forget to include a healthy lifestyle by incorporating exercise and a proper diet. By making significant changes in your life, you reduce stress and add value to your life. Remember those lasting impressions start from within. So strive to adapt to habits that will leave an impact in ages to come.

Butterfly Effect

Learn to embrace the butterfly effect concept. This notion speaks of little things that lead to massive results. The idea is created from the butterfly story. Its flapping wings can influence a hurricane in a different part of the world as little as it is. The small things we do in life can create the same impact. The implication is felt in our personal lives and the universe too. If it is a positive deed, the world benefits from it. The universe is not biased in reciprocating back. If we give it value, that is precisely what it offers back or even much more. Here are eight approaches to help you introduce value in life.

Do Not Give Up

Naturally, there is always the fear of the unknown. Our upbringing can make us rigid to change. This approach can block good tidings along the way. When you create value, everything around you changes. This does not happen overnight. You have to focus ahead and not reel back to the stagnant zones. Through the journey, you may realize that there are things that you need to do away with. Old beliefs and approaches to life should get out of the bucket list. Open your mind to welcome positive energy. The process can get more protracted than we assume. Do not fret if success is not achieved as you had anticipated. Remember, that good things come in small doses. When you feel uncertain, do not stop. Light is just around the corner.

Embrace Kindness and Teamwork

Building value is more about creating solid relationships. If you relate well with others, the positive energy will reflect in your life. Start by taking an interest in the people you meet. Learn to connect well with other people and avoid foul language. Detach your personal experiences from others. We are not cut from the cloth; we should work as a team and not pull each other down. Occasionally, you may get forced to drop some people along the way. The bottom line is to finish the race successfully and not hold on to people who are blocking the path.

Keep Your Mind Busy

There is a popular term that says that an idle mind is the devil's workshop. There might be some truth to the statement. Our reasons are vital in all the decisions we make. Through it, we create strategies and adjustments needed. If we surround ourselves with negative energy, we lack the will power to progress. Sometimes our breakthroughs lie in our minds and not on actual events and meetings. You can make a million-dollar decision while relaxing on your couch. The trick is to keep our minds alert and away from things that cloud it. Feed it with empowering content; you can grab a journal, sneak into a business blog. Refrain from addictive activities like playing candy crush. Instead, take a walk and breathe in the fresh air. Sooner, you will realize an increased focus and efficiency in your life. You will relate better with those close to you and get more in sync with your needs.

Block Criticism

As we strive to improve our lives, we should not beat ourselves too much. Life is not about competition. People receive their breakthroughs at different seasons of life. Remember, the final reward is on those who are making a change. It does not matter how small it seems. When you attempt a new idea, it is your small contribution to the world. Sometimes, people may not welcome them well. Critics and haters are on standby for downfalls. We should learn to give ourselves credit for the things we do. It is comforting to know that through our defenselessness, we can stand stronger again. Inaccuracy should help us adjust and not break us. With that approach, you will manage to face the challenges steadfastly.

Discover Yourself

Life is such an exciting journey when you take the right steps. It is more exciting to discover yourself. Self-reflection opens up internal energy that we share with the world. By introducing this aspect, you realize some characteristics that you never knew you had. It empowers you to prioritize the important things in your life. Surprisingly, due to the empowerment, some negative people in your life might disappear. As a result, you get to appreciate yourself more, and face the world from a different perspective.

Follow Your Heart

In some instances, surroundings can cloud our judgments. Through the people and situations in our lives, our opinions may get distracted. It is a very confusing moment when you are not able to make clear conclusions. It only creates a counterfeit sense of security. To penetrate, you need to discover the certainty of your feelings. Sometimes, our instincts are the guidelines and the key to our success. This accomplishment requires patience and courage. If you manage to stand firmly on your decisions, success is beckoning. Learn to listen to your inner person and not get carried away by emotions. If you work to connect your heart and strength of mind, you will value yourself more.

Keep Off From Old Destructive Behaviors

Through the journey of life, you can count your profits and losses. The mistakes you made were probably due to some misguided steps. Some of them negatively affected your self-esteem and left you in shame. In such situations, remember that it is normal to make mistakes. Learn from them and move forward. If an old lousy habit reoccurs, you need to understand what triggers it. You may be having trouble with drinking alcohol. But it only happens when you meet certain friends. That should be the wake-up call. If you can manage to avoid these people, then your problem is solved. It requires a lot of grace to drop old practices. You only need to view the destructive effect on your life and make a firm decision.

Create a Healthy Regime

You will only manage to make progress in life if your mind and body are in good shape. Making reliable decisions requires a clear mind and a full stomach. We all know how our mind wanders away while hungry. A balanced diet is a foundation for a healthy lifestyle. Not only does it keep you away from illnesses, but it also gives you energy. Greens should be included in all meals to prevent vitamin deficiency sicknesses. Do not forget to add carbohydrates and vitamins. Make sure to take at least eight glasses of water. It will clear your skin and keep you away from headaches. Introduce relaxing regimes like walking, and massages. Through these therapeutic measures, you will create an empire to face the world.

5 POINTS I HAVE LEARNED IN MY JOURNEY TO GOING GLOBAL

1 ______________________________

____

2 ______________________________

____

3 ______________________________

____

4 ______________________________

____

5 ______________________________

____

CHAPTER 8

Sharing Value And Experiences With Others.

VALUES ARE WHAT IS valued or esteemed such as morals or a belief system while experience is the knowledge gathered over a period of time. Christian values and experiences are beneficial if shared.

Before someone shares their experience and values they must put this in to consideration.

Study first the value or experience you intend to share.
This is to determine whether the value or experience is fit for sharing. Some values or experiences to our view may look good but when shared to others may not make sense or be applicable to the group that it is being shared with.

This means that we should first study who are the recipients of what we need to share. The shared value or experience should be for the aim of edifying or bringing a change to the people that you are sharing with. If the value or experience is irrelevant there is no need of wasting time to share it.

Apostle Paul shares his experience with the church in Corinth about the generosity of the Church in Macedonian. Paul shares this not as a way of comparison but to challenge the church in Corinth that they can do better than the church in Macedonia because they had the financial potential.

> Moreover, brethren, we make known to you the grace of God bestowed on the churches of Macedonia: that in a great trial of affliction the abundance of their joy and their deep poverty abounded in the riches of their liberality. For I bear witness that according to their ability, yes, and beyond their ability, they were freely willing, imploring us with much urgency that we would receive the gift and the fellowship of the ministering to the saints. And not only as we had hoped, but they first gave themselves to the Lord, and then to us by the will of God. So we urged Titus, that as he had begun, so he would also complete this grace in you as well. ***But as you abound in everything—in faith, in speech, in knowledge, in all diligence, and in your love for us—see that you abound in this grace also.*** (2 Corinthians 8: 1-7).

See the wisdom Apostle Paul uses when he finishing talking about his experience with the church in Macedonia, he finishes by encouraging them that as they continue abounding in everything they should be careful also to abound in the grace of giving.

Find out which part of your experience is worth sharing.

Not all your experience is worth sharing. You should only share which part of your experience that will benefit the body of Christ. For instance, we once attended a service of a certain local church on a Sunday. The Preacher sharing the word was a lady who was the pastor of that congregation.

She was the main preacher of the day. She started preaching very well but at a point she diverted and started talking about how she was evil before she got born again. She took the better part of the sermon in sharing how about her evil acts in night clubs and all sorts of evil etc.

Okay, it is not bad or evil for someone to share their experience especially where God rescued them from. But in your experience God should be magnified in all ways.

Apostle Paul had an evil past which he shares that he can't rejoice in it. What he is now focused on is the excellence of the knowledge of Christ His Lord.

> Though I also might have confidence in the flesh. If anyone else thinks he may have confidence in the flesh, I more so: circumcised the eighth day, of the stock of Israel, of the tribe of Benjamin, a Hebrew of the Hebrews; concerning the law, a Pharisee; concerning zeal, persecuting the church; concerning the righteousness which is in the law, blameless. But what things were gain to me, these I have counted loss for Christ. Yet indeed I also count all things loss for

> the excellence of the knowledge of Christ Jesus my Lord, for whom I have suffered the loss of all things, and count them as rubbish, that I may gain Christ (Philippians 3:4-8)

After studying keenly the types of values or experiences that we are about to share and after finding out which part is worth sharing we should find out the way we should share it.

Finding how to share the value or experience.

This is more of your presentation of what is needed to be shared. One may have a good value or experience to share but fail on the presentation process. This calls for someone who is presenting the experience or values to study and gain knowledge on the presentation tactics. So a lot of time and resources should be invested in this.

IMPORTANCE OF SHARING YOUR VALUES AND EXPERIENCES WITH OTHERS.

a) It leads to edification.

When correct values and experiences are shared well they lead to edification. Leaders should be ready to share their success stories to the ones that they are leading not as a way of showing off but to edify them.

The miraculous opening of the prison door when Paul and Silas were in prison created a good avenue of the people around them developing faith in God and the gospel that the Apostle were preaching.

The experience brought salvation to the Jailer and his family. Had Paul and Silas not shared the experience on what power set them free the Jailer couldn't have received the gospel and got born again.

Immediately after the release of Paul and Silas from prison, they straight away went to the house of Lydia where they continued sharing their experience and edified those that were in the house.

> **and they went out of the prison and entered the house of Lydia; and when they had seen the brethren, they encouraged them and departed. (Acts 16:40)**

b) It leads to perfection.

They say wise people learn from the experiences of others. When leaders share what they have gone through to the point where they are currently, it will teach others on the values that they should embrace if they are willing to follow the path to succeed.

They will avoid the mistakes that others who were before them made and try to follow the correct paths to reach the level they want. All the Old Testament incidents and stories are a good experience that the church has been presented to by the word of God.

If anyone would love to live a perfect life, they will follow the good choices that the people who succeeded in the Old Testament did. The story of Joseph in the Old Testament is enough experience that one can learn from it and make up their mind that they will be determined at all cost to avoid evil if they will need to succeed and achieve their dreams.

On the other hand, the story of Samson shows how disobedience and wrong choices can ruin someone's life. Samson's experience as shared by the word of God is enough to make someone know the consequences of disobedience and sin.

There are many stories written both in the Old Testament and the New Testament that can teach someone how to live a life that honors God. That is why the Bible says.

> **For whatever things were written before were written for our learning, that we through the patience and comfort of the Scriptures might have hope. (Romans 15:4)**

> **All Scripture is given by inspiration of God, and is profitable for doctrine, for reproof, for correction, for instruction in righteousness, that the man of God may be complete, thoroughly equipped for every good work. (2 Timothy 3:16-17)**

It is a form of mentorship.

One of the ways of mentoring someone is to share your values and experiences with them. Mentees will always learn from how their mentor used to do. That is to why in the beginning we discussed on how the mentor should know what to share and what not to as human beings are not perfect and are bound to errors.

In the story of King David there are good values that we can learn from his life like the life of worship that he had. But even as we try to look up to King David we will find out that there were areas that he made mistakes in life. Those are the areas that when we study King David's life we should try to avoid at all cost.

Timothy who was the mentee of Apostle Paul not only learned the doctrine that Apostle Paul taught but also he learned the way of life that Paul lived. The experience of Apostle Paul in ministry was enough to usher Timothy into ministry. These are the words he used to encourage him.

> ***But you have carefully followed my doctrine, manner of life, purpose, faith, longsuffering, love, perseverance, persecutions, afflictions, which happened to me at Antioch, at Iconium, at Lystra—what persecutions I endured.*** And out of them all the Lord delivered me. Yes, and all who desire to live godly in Christ Jesus will suffer persecution. But evil men and impostors will grow worse and worse, deceiving and being deceived. But you must continue in the things which you have learned and been assured of, knowing from whom you have learned them, and that from childhood you have known the Holy Scriptures, which are able to make you wise for salvation through faith which is in Christ Jesus. (2 Timothy 3:10-15)

5 POINTS I HAVE LEARNED IN MY JOURNEY TO GOING GLOBAL

1 ______________________________

____

2 ______________________________

____

3 ______________________________

____

4 ______________________________

____

5 ______________________________

____

CHAPTER 9

Always Be A Learner

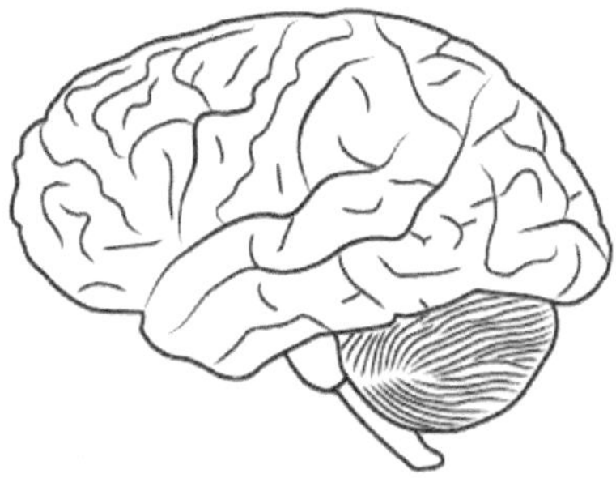

GOD STRUCTURED LIFE AS a school, and we are all learners. Learning is essential to living. There are new lessons every day for us to learn. Knowledge keeps increasing, and we must not be ignorant. Great people in the world are known to be great readers. We can never know too much. The more we learn, the more we realize there is more for us to learn. Learning should be continuous for us, as much as we live.

Learning enriches our minds, and open doors to new thinking, fresh perspectives and new opportunities. To be successful, we cannot overestimate the need to learn continuously. As long as there is room for improvement, there is room for learning. When we learn, we not only become informed, we get transformed into better versions of ourselves. Learning new things can initiate personal, professional and organizational growth. In fact, the book of Proverbs contains wise words that establish the need and benefit of learning.

> **"How much better to get wisdom than gold, to get insight than silver" (Proverbs 16:16 NIV)**

Gold is good, but it is better to get wisdom. However, it is best to get both wisdom and gold. Silver is good, but it is better to get insight. However, it is best to get both insight and silver. The reason wisdom is better than gold is that a wise man who has gold can multiply the gold, but a man who lacks wisdom will lose his gold because of ignorance. It takes wisdom to learn about what you do not know. Ignorance and folly go together. It is folly to know you do not know, yet not seek to know.

> **"Let the wise listen and add to their learning, and the one who understands obtain guidance" (Proverbs 1:5 NIV)**

It takes a wise man to see the need to listen and learn. There is no wise man who could not desire to learn. A wise man can learn from the aged, colleagues, friends, foes, parents and even young children. There is no limit to learning, and there is no standard about the personality of our teachers. Anyone can teach us what we do not know.

"The mind of the prudent is ever getting knowledge, and the ear of the wise is ever seeking (inquiring for and craving) knowledge" (Proverbs 18:15 AMP).

Wisdom is ever seeking to learn. Anyone who does not seek to know is a fool. We must maintain a heart posture that seeks to learn always. Learning positions us for wisdom. The Bible says,

"Study and be eager and do your utmost to present yourself to God approved (tested by trial), a workman who has no cause to be ashamed, correctly analyzing and accurately dividing [rightly handling and skillfully teaching] the Word of Truth" (2 Timothy 2:15 AMP).

As leaders, we are God's workmen, and it is required of us to be skillful in our handling of the Word of God and the things of God. We should be able to know the truth so well that we can identify false teachings and erroneous philosophies. We must be eager to study, search and research the truth about God, and Kingdom operations such that we can master the art of living the God-life with so much wisdom regarding all that pertain to life and Godliness.

The Bible says,

'...the people who know their God shall prove themselves strong and shall stand firm and do exploits [for God]' (Daniel 11:32).

When we learn about God, we get strengthened and empowered to do exploits. When we know Christ, and in Him dwells the fullness of God bodily. When we become committed to pursuing the knowledge of God through Christ, we find limitless strength. The Bible consists of stories about men and women who were feeble and frail, but encountered God and were empowered to do mighty things for God.

We know that the knowledge grows; even the knowledge of God grows. It is part of the features of the last days that knowledge shall increase (Daniel 12:4), so we should not be in the twenty-first century, and not update our knowledge of God's moves, will and plans for our generation. We must maintain a heart that seeks to know more, especially in areas God needs us.

While we learn, we should not become too vain in our learning. The Bible talks about some people who learn, but never come to know the truth. The Bible says,

> **"Always learning but never able to come to a knowledge of the truth" (2 Timothy 3:7 NIV)**

> **"Furthermore, just as they did not think it worthwhile to retain the knowledge of God, so God gave them over to a depraved mind, so that they do what ought not to be done" (Romans 1:28 NIV).**

These people commit themselves to learning, but rejected the knowledge of God, so they never come to realize the truth. Today, we see them, people living godless lives, and doing things that are not right. When a man has knowledge without knowing the truth, he remains in darkness, in the bondage of knowledge.

The end product of learning is the truth. The truth we know is capable of giving us liberty. When you know something, you are delivered from the bondage of ignorance. When you know the truth about finance, relationship, business and leadership, you become free from the darkness of ignorance in that aspect. The greatest truth is to know and accept Christ as Savior and Lord. This truth liberates us and brings us into the marvelous light, and the more truth we know, the more light we embody.

Having established the need to be open to learning more about God, we need to establish the need to consistently learn more for personal, professional and business development and productivity. You need to actively look forward to learning new things. Our physical development requires food; however, all other development will only be possible by learning.

Benefits of learning

Learning gives you an advantage. With the advent of digital technology, many things have changed, even the skills on demand. To adapt to the ever dynamic world of ours, we must keep learning, relearning and unlearning.

Learning can be difficult and sometimes demanding. It can even be frustrating if we are not getting things right. Although learning is hard, there is nothing more fulfilling than achieving your goals and pursuits. The feeling of satisfaction is good for happiness. The more we achieve our goals, the happier we become. Learning fosters happiness in the long run.

Learning helps you gain mastery. When you learn, you will have opportunities to teach others who do not know, and that way, you will be able to master your skill, update your knowledge and get better as a person in what you do.

As global Christians, we must be committed to learning so we may rise to the position of leadership. The learning culture should be part of our lives. We saw this in Jesus Christ when He was young. The Bible says,

> **"After three days they found him in the temple courts, sitting among the teachers, listening to them and asking them questions" (Luke 2:46 NIV).**

We must be ready to overcome arrogance, anxiety and self-satisfaction if we want to become better as a person and in what we do. What are you learning? What have you learned that needs to be unlearned? What have you unlearn that needs to be relearned?

Apostle Paul after doing exploits for God, establishing churches and impacting lives came to a point where he felt there is yet more for him to learn. The Bible says,

> **"What is more, I consider everything a loss because of the surpassing worth of knowing Christ Jesus my Lord, for whose sake I have lost all things. I consider them garbage that I may gain Christ and be found in him, not having a righteousness of my own that comes from the law, but that which is through faith in Christ – the righteousness of my own that comes from God on the basis of faith. I want to know Christ – yes, to know the power of his resurrection and participation in his sufferings, becoming like him in his death, and so, somehow, attaining to the resurrection from the dead. Not that I have already obtained all this, or have already arrived at my goal, but I press on to take hold of that for which Christ Jesus took**

hold of me. Brothers and sisters, I do not consider myself yet to have taken hold of it. But one thing I do: forgetting what is behind and straining toward what is ahead, I press on toward the goal to win the prize for which God has called me heavenward in Christ Jesus" (Philippians 3:8- 14 NIV).

As Christians, we are Disciples of Christ. The meaning of the Greek word for disciple is 'learner'. The Discipleship we are called into is a lifelong learning process. Jesus told the disciples,

"Come to me, all who labor and are heavy laden, and I will give you rest. Take my yoke upon you, and learn from me, for I am gentle and lowly in heart, and you will find rest for your souls. For my yoke is easy, and my burden is light" (Matthew 11:28 ESV)

Generally, it is believed that anyone who stops learning starts dying. It will not be wrong to say that learning is living. Lifelong learning is not a mere concept, it should be culture. As long as we live, we live to learn. We can learn new habits, attitudes and skills, establish new friendships, discover new things, explore fresh things and read new books. These things can create our journey of learning. Learning should not be restricted to the walls of the classroom. We should be able to learn, anywhere and everywhere, as long as there is value in what we are learning.

How to learn continuously

- Willingness to learn: Learning cannot be forced on you; you must be willing to learn. Willingness gives you the internal drive to do whatever it takes to learn. Children are known to be curious learners. They ask questions, and are never ashamed about asking, even though their questions are sometimes funny. As we grow, many of us lose willingness and curiosity, which are crucial to learning. Willingness opens us up to learning new things.

- Eagerness or enthusiasm: It is believed that enthusiasm is the energy of young children that helps them to be curious, creative and successful. Naturally, we all had enthusiasm while we were children, but as we grew, we lost it with the consciousness of adulthood. Often, this translates to arrogance, and prevents us from learning new things. This is why we often avoid learning some things by saying 'the younger ones will learn them'. Learning is active, and will only be effective if we are eager to learn. Truth is, we cannot be eager to learn everything, but we should sustain enthusiasm to learn some things.

- Practice what you learn: When you practice what you learn, and you realize the impact on your life, you would be compelled to learn more. The Bible encourages us to be doers, and not hearers alone. Do not just learn, ensure you act.

Every day is an opportunity to learn. God has designed each day for us to learn new things. Your life is unique, and God designed each day as a means to bring you into a new level of awareness, and make you better. The Word of God is one of God's instruments for our transformation. He also uses our everyday life experiences, people and situations to make us learn.

As a leader and entrepreneur, you must be able to learn God's wisdom for your life and business. Your relationship with God is an advantage for your life and business. The higher the ladder of success, influence and greatness you climb, the more you must be open to learning. Learning culture is a global culture for global leaders and entrepreneurs.

5 POINTS I HAVE LEARNED IN MY JOURNEY TO GOING GLOBAL

1 ______________________________

____

2 ______________________________

____

3 ______________________________

____

4 ______________________________

____

5 ______________________________

____

CHAPTER 10

Always Giving

"Is not this the kind of fasting I have chosen: to loose the chains of injustice and untie the cords of the yoke, to set the oppressed go free and break every yoke? Is it not to share your food with the hungry and to provide the poor wanderer with shelter – when you see the naked, to clothe them, and not to turn away from your own flesh and blood?" (Isaiah 58:6-7 NIV)

GIVING IS NOT ONLY an instruction from God, it is a lifestyle, and God exemplified this by giving us Jesus Christ to die for our sins, and bridge the gap between us and Him as the only way. We are expected to give justice by breaking the chains of injustice, give freedom by untying the cords of yoke and relieve those who are a burden. Also, we are to give food to those who are hungry, shelter to those who are homeless, and cloth to those who are naked.

In your journey to becoming a global leader, giving should be a part of you. It is a very important principle in the Kingdom of God. Giving is God's design, and He structured it in a way that both the giver and receiver are blessed. There cannot be genuine love without benevolence. The Bible says,

> **"In everything I did, I showed you that by this kind of hard work we must help the weak, remembering the words of Lord Jesus himself said: 'It is more blessed to give than to receive'" (Acts 20:35 NIV).**

One of the most profound quotes was given by Mother Theresa: "Never worry about numbers. Help one person at a time, and always start with the person nearest you". Giving creates more blessings for the giver. The Bible says,

> **"Those who give to the poor will lack nothing, but those who close their eyes to them receive many curses" (Proverbs 28:27 NIV).**

There is wisdom and blessing in giving. The more we give, the more we have, and the more we rise. When we check through both the Old Testament and the New Testament, we will see the outcome of benevolent giving. From the scriptures, we are taught and inspired to give benevolently and also with the right mindset and motivation.

Giving demands faith. We often find it difficult without faith. This is because our logic tends to calculate the things we need to use our funds for, and reasons we can give when we have more. Truth is, there will always be needs, but when we give out of faith in God and hope in love, we will always have more. Giving is God's way of showing how much we trust Him. God tried Abraham's faith by instructing him to offer up Isaac.

God is a giver. The Bible says,

> **"For God so loved the world that he gave his one and only Son, that whoever believes in him shall not perish but have eternal life" (John 3:16 NIV).**

God gave Jesus out of love. We are to be like our Heavenly Father by giving out of love. There cannot be genuine love without giving. Giving is one of the ways to demonstrate genuine love. It is also important to understand that giving is difficult without trust. When we desire to give, there is often something to compete with our resources, but when we trust God enough, we will be able to give without restraint. The Bible says,

> **"Trust in the Lord with all your heart and lean not on your own understanding; in all your ways submit to him, and he will make your paths straight. Do not be wise in your own eyes; fear the Lord and shun evil." (Proverbs 3:5-7 NIV).**

When it comes to giving, we are to trust God with all our heart. Do not lean on your understanding to give, because of the tendency of your mind to get fixed on your needs. When you are tempted to lean on your understanding, remember what the Scriptures say about giving so that you can lean on the understanding of God's Word. Your understanding of the situation you are in may hinder your giving. Your understanding of your personal needs and the need to prepare for unforeseen circumstances can rob you of the blessing of giving.

Blessings of giving

We cannot exhaust the blessings that accompany giving, but we will go through some as written in the Bible. After we are told to help those in oppression, give to the poor and clothe the naked, the Scriptures talk about the blessings that follow. The Bible says,

> **"Then your light will break forth like the dawn, and your healing will quickly appear; then your righteousness will go before you, and the glory of the Lord will be your rear guard. Then you will call, and the Lord will answer; you will cry for help, and he will say: Here am I. "If you do away with the yoke of oppression. With the pointing finger and malicious talk" (Isaiah 58:8-9 NIV)**

When you give, your light will break forth like dawn, your healing will quickly appear, and your righteousness will go before you, and the glory of the Lord will be your rear guard. Giving opens up to new blessings, such that is new like the breaking of a new day. Giving can facilitate healing for the giver. Giving brings us closer to God such that when we call, He answers. Giving gives us the confidence to call for help, and God will show up.

The Bible says,

> **"Give, and it will be given to you. A good measure, pressed down, shaken together and running over, will be poured into your lap. For with the measure you use, it will be measured to you" (Luke 6:38 NIV).**

Giving prepares us to receive. The way to get blessed is to bless others. When we give, we get more than the measure we give. In God's infinite wisdom, He structured His measurement in a way that givers get to receive more than they gave.

One of the wonderful things about giving is that it does not have to do with money alone. You can give yourself by volunteering or serving. You can give time, materials and even counsel. When it comes to giving, the reward is not always instantaneous. Generally, it is believed that givers never lack.

> **"Let us not become weary in doing good, for at the proper time we will reap a harvest if we do not give up" (Galatians 6:9 NIV).**

We should not be weary in doing good and in giving, because there is always harvest time. Giving is more like sowing seeds, if we do not give up, we will reap a harvest. Also, we need to remember that the quality and quantity of our giving will determine the quality and quantity of our harvest. The Bible says,

> **"Remember this: Whoever sows sparingly will also reap sparingly, and whoever sows generously will also reap generously" (2 Corinthians 9:6 NIV).**

If we are not receiving as we expect, we should examine our giving and the heart from which we give. We are not to give out of weariness. There is a proper time that comes with harvest for those who do not become weary in doing good and giving. As an entrepreneur, giving can be the key to the door to your abundance. As a leader, giving may be the remaining part of the password to unlock your access to more platforms.

As Christians, we have trivialized giving when it comes to certain areas of our life. We have an assumption that it is bribing our way through. This is not true. The Bible says,

> **"A gift opens the way and ushers the giver into the presence of the great" (Proverbs 18:16 NIV).**

Your gift can pave the way to the midst of great people. Giving can open a way to access a new circle of friends. Giving can usher you in to receive a contract or seal a deal. God desires to have many sons; He gave Christ to the world and graciously by the time of harvest, we will definitely have many sons in God's Kingdom. Whatever we desire more, when we give it, it comes back more.

5 POINTS I HAVE LEARNED IN MY JOURNEY TO GOING GLOBAL

1 ______________________________

____

2 ______________________________

____

3 ______________________________

____

4 ______________________________

____

5 ______________________________

____

CHAPTER 11

Investing Financially Into Others

CHRISTIANITY IS NOT ABOUT oneself but for the benefit of others. Every gift that God gives the church should be of the benefit of the entire body of Jesus Christ.

> And there are diversities of activities, but it is the same God who works all in all. But the manifestation of the Spirit is given to each one ***for the profit of all*** (1 Corinthians 12:6-7).

When God blesses someone in the body of Christ with finances, it is not for his benefit but for the benefit of the people around them. And that is what we call Christian service.

Believers in the early church displayed an exemplary character that is highly recommendable. From the book of Acts, you see how they shared all that they had that no one lacked in their midst.

Look at how the Bible describes them; *Now all who believed were together, and had all things in common, and sold their possessions and goods, and divided them among all, as anyone had need.* (Acts 2:44-45).

Reasons for investing financially into others.

We should invest in others financially because:

a) We are called to serve one another.

One principle of a Christian is to serve one another. Jesus Christ showed this act of service practically by washing the feet of His disciples.

> So when He had washed their feet, taken His garments, and sat down again, He said to them, "Do you know what I have done to you? You call Me Teacher and Lord, and you say well, for so I am. If I then, your Lord and Teacher, have washed your feet, you also ought to wash one another's feet. For I have given you an example, that you should do as I have done to you. Most assuredly, I say to you, a servant is not greater than his master; nor is he who is sent greater than he who sent him. If you know these things, blessed are you if you do them. (John 13:12-17).

b) It is service to God.

It is God who enables someone to increase in wealth. No one create wealth by their own power both believers and non-believers. "*And you shall remember the Lord your God,* ***for it is he who gives you power to get wealth,*** *that He may establish His covenant which He swore to your fathers, as it is this day.*(Deuteronomy 8 :18).

When one realizes this they will not find it hard to invest financially in others. As Jesus Christ said that whatever we do to the little ones we are doing unto Him.

> **"Then the righteous will answer Him, saying, 'Lord, when did we see You hungry and feed You, or thirsty and give You drink? When did we see You a stranger and take You in, or naked and clothe You? Or when did we see You sick, or in prison, and come to You?' And the King will answer and say to them, *'Assuredly, I say to you, inasmuch as you did it to one of the least of these My brethren, you did it to Me.'* (Matthew 25:37-40).**

c) It is creating an investment in heaven.

When we stand with others financially, we are creating our investment in heaven. That is why the Bible says; *He who has pity on the poor lends to the Lord,*

> **And He will pay back what he has given. (Proverbs 19:17).**

There is no one that wouldn't want to make an investment in heaven, as this earth is not our own and we are just sojourners.

Heaven is our permanent dwelling place, a place that we will dwell forever. Therefore, it is good to invest in heaven than on this earth.

> "Do not lay up for yourselves treasures on earth, where moth and rust destroy and where thieves break in and steal; but lay up for yourselves treasures in heaven, where neither moth nor rust destroys and where thieves do not break in and steal. For where your treasure is, there your heart will be also. (Mathew 6:19-21).

> And let us not grow weary while doing good, for in due season we shall reap if we do not lose heart. Therefore, as we have opportunity, let us do good to all, especially to those who are of the household of faith. (Galatians 6:9-10)

d) It is a way of being shrewd.

Shrewdness is a way of showing clever resourcefulness in practical matters. To teach this principle Jesus Christ had to teach this parable.

> He also said to His disciples: "There was a certain rich man who had a steward, and an accusation was brought to him that this man was wasting his goods. So he called him and said to him, 'What is this I hear about you? Give an account of your stewardship, for you can no longer be steward. 'Then the steward said within himself, 'What shall I do? For my master is taking the stewardship away from me. I cannot dig; I am ashamed to beg. I have resolved what to do, that when I am put out of the stewardship, they may receive me into their houses. 'So he called every one of his master's debtors to him, and said to the first, 'How much do you owe my master?' And he said,

> 'A hundred measures of oil.' So he said to him, 'Take your bill, and sit down quickly and write fifty. 'Then he said to another, 'And how much do you owe?' So he said, 'A hundred measures of wheat.' And he said to him, 'Take your bill, and write eighty.' So the master commended the unjust steward because he had dealt shrewdly. For the sons of this world are more shrewd in their generation than the sons of light. "And I say to you, make friends for yourselves by unrighteous mammon, that when you fail, they may receive you into an everlasting home. (Luke 16:1-9)

I don't know why Jesus Christ had to use a wrong example to teach a biblical principle. Just to explain this parable. The rich man represents God and the shrewd steward is represents any human being.

The shrewd steward is very wise with his funds, when he hears that his master is taking the stewardship from him (realizing his days on the earth are few) he decides to invest in people who will help him when he will not be able to dig so he calls his master's debtors and uses his money to invest in them. This is compared to investing in God's work. He knows very well that it is not in vain. And one day he will get back what he invested. This is how investing financially in others is beneficial.

e) It is a way of bearing one another's burden.

Christians are called upon to bear one another's burden in all aspects. When the church in Jerusalem was facing financial challenges the Macedonian church played a very big role in making sure that the needs of the church in Jerusalem are met.

> Moreover, brethren, we make known to you the grace of God bestowed on the churches of Macedonia: that in a great trial of affliction the abundance of their joy and their deep poverty abounded in the riches of their liberality. For I bear witness that according to their ability, yes, and beyond their ability, they were freely willing, imploring us with much urgency that we would receive the gift and the fellowship of the ministering to the saints. And not only as we had hoped, but they first gave themselves to the Lord, and then to us by the will of God. (2 Corinthians 8:5).

The Bible says that the church in Macedonia gave beyond their ability this means they took the sufferings of the church in Jerusalem as theirs and made sure that they had what they needed.

Apostle Paul was writing this letter to the church in Corinth because they could help the church in Jerusalem but were not willing to do that. He challenges them so that they can learn a good example from the Macedonians.

> So let each one give as he purposes in his heart, not grudgingly or of necessity; for God loves a cheerful giver. And God is able to make all grace abound toward you, that you, always having all sufficiency in all things, may have an abundance for every good work. (2 Corinthians 9: 7-8)

f) It is the Outworking of love.

Finally, when we invest financially in others it is an act of extending love to our fellow brethren as God commands us

By this we know love, because He laid down His life for us. And we also ought to lay down our lives for the brethren. But whoever has this world's goods, and sees his brother in need, and shuts up his heart from him, how does the love of God abide in him? (1 John 3:16-17)

5 POINTS I HAVE LEARNED IN MY JOURNEY TO GOING GLOBAL

1 ______________________________

____

2 ______________________________

____

3 ______________________________

____

4 ______________________________

____

5 ______________________________

____

CHAPTER 12

Praying For Nations

"And pray in the Spirit on all occasions with all kinds of prayers and requests. With this in mind, be alert and always keep on praying for all the Lord's people" (Ephesians 6:18 NIV)

PRAYER IS A POWERFUL weapon God gave His people to engage God and His power, accomplish the purposes of the Kingdom and birth extraordinary results. Prayer is beyond the ritual of asking and seeking, it also creates a strong union between man and God. When we labor, we take responsibility, but when we pray, God takes responsibility.

The Holy Scripture contains stories of people who prayed and got response from Heaven. If there is a man who can pray, we should be rest assured that there is a God to answer. The people of God should pray to God not only during difficult times, to seek help, leading and guidance, but also during good times to know and do God's will.

Since we know we are sent to all nations, it is our responsibility to pray for nations. We are called to the ministry of prayer. The secret of Christians lies in their secret place. A secret place is the place of prayer, power and the Word. As humans, we are limited in our scope, power, possibility and wisdom, and we pray to expand our limits by engaging the limitless scope, power, possibility and wisdom of God.

When the disciples came to Jesus to teach them how to pray, the first thing He mentioned was to acknowledge God as our Father. The Bible says,

> **"He said to them, "When you pray, say: "Father, hallowed be your name, your kingdom come." (Luke 11:2 NIV)**

God is our Father. He loves us so much that He gave us His precious beloved Son Jesus.

> **"He who did not spare his own Son, but gave him up for us all – how will he not also, along with him, graciously give us all things?" (Romans 8:32 NIV)**

God has given us the greatest gift, His Son, and when we ask for anything, how will He not give us all things? This is the confidence we should have when we pray. God did not spare Jesus, what will He spare to give us joy, satisfaction and fulfillment?

The Bible says.

> **"I urge, then, first of all, that petitions, prayers, intercession and thanksgiving be made for all people – for kings and all those in authority, that we may live peaceful and quiet lives in all godliness and holiness" (1 Timothy 1:1-2 NIV).**

Petition is asking for something from God. Prayer is a means of communication with God. Intercession is praying on behalf of others. Thanksgiving is an expression of gratitude to God.

Praying for nations can come in different ways. We can decide to pray for missionaries who sacrifice to take the Gospel to the nations of the world. We can also decide to pray for nations in crises, war, poverty and natural disaster. No matter where you are, your voice can go beyond your community and country to the end of the earth. God needs a partner with whom He can discuss His heart desires, and who can stand in the gap in the place of prayer. The Bible says,

> **"I looked for someone among them who would build up the wall and stand before me in the gap on behalf of the land so I would not have to destroy it, but I found no one" (Ezekiel 22:30 NIV).**

We have Christians in every nation of the earth. Prayer has the power to change things by bringing Heaven to interfere and intervene in the matters on earth.

We are not to pray for some men, few men but for all men. Leadership demands that we pray and intercede for all men, known and unknown, near and far away. We must engage in petitions, prayers, intercession and thanksgiving for everyone.

This responsibility will enlarge our scope beyond our immediate sphere. It is quite easy to pray for members of your family, friends and brethren, but as global leaders, we need to know that we have family members, friends and family members in other nations of the world. We are part of God's family, and every Christian is our sibling.

As leaders, we will have followers and fans in other nations of the world, who are passionate about the grace and ministry that God has assigned to us. This brings us to see the need to pray for nations. Nations are more than countries. When we talk about nations, nations mean people from different walks of life.

The Bible says,

> **"You're familiar with the old written law, 'Love your friend,' and its unwritten companion, 'Hate your enemy.' I'm challenging that. I'm telling you to love your enemies. Let them bring out the best in you, not the worst. When someone gives you a hard time, respond with the energies of prayer, for then you are working out of your true selves, your God-created selves. This is what God does. He gives his best—the sun to warm and the rain to nourish—to everyone, regardless: the good and bad, the nice and nasty. If all you do is love the lovable, do you expect a bonus? Anybody can do that. If you simply say hello to those who greet you, do you expect a medal? Any run-of-the-mill sinner does that." (Matthew 5:43-47 MSG).**

We should pray, not just for our friends, for our enemies as well. We must learn to pray deliberately for all men. We should pray for those who need to come into the light of the Gospel and become saved, for neighbors and for coworkers. Also, we should pray for Christian leaders in all spheres. When we do this, we come into the light of God's leadership and responsibility as a joint worker of God.

> **"For kings and all who are in positions of authority or high responsibility, that [outwardly] we may pass a quiet and undisturbed life [and inwardly] a peaceable one in all godliness and holiness" (1 Timothy 2:2 AMP).**

We should not just limit our prayers to Christian leaders, we should also pray for the government and rulers. We must pray for God to direct their hearts to make policies that will favor Christian values and also the advancement of God's Kingdom. An ungodly leader will propagate the ungodly agenda. So we must pray that God sits on the throne of every nation of the world. We pray for them so that we may live peaceful lives and serve God to all pleasing.

> **"This is good, and pleases God our Savior, who wants all people to be saved and to come to a knowledge of the truth" (2 Timothy 2:3-4 NIV).**

The paramount thing an unbelieving leader needs is not wisdom, but Christ. When we pray for leaders, we should direct our prayer towards the need for them to be saved. Ultimately, our objective is to bring them to come under the leadership and authority of Christ, so that their activities and laws can give room for the propagation of the Gospel. Irrespective of status, class or position, God desires that all men become saved.

Aside salvation, God also desires that all men come to the knowledge of truth. This is very important because the knowledge of truth liberates a man from the power of darkness, sin and worldliness. The Bible says,

> **"Then you will know the truth, and the truth will set you free" (John 8:32 NIV).**

The knowledge of Christ and His sacrifice to bring salvation to mankind is the first truth man needs to be saved. However, man needs to grow in grace and in the knowledge of God so that he may come into the light of his place and assignment in God's agenda and plan.

God told us to ask for nations for heritage. The Bible says,

> **"Ask me, and I will make the nations your inheritance, the ends of the earth your possession" (Psalms 2:4 NIV).**

How shall we ask for nations if we do not pray for nations? The world needs daring Christians who would win their industries, societies, spheres, markets, businesses, cultures and internet for the Lord. We must not be frightened or distracted to fulfill God's mandate.

5 POINTS I HAVE LEARNED IN MY JOURNEY TO GOING GLOBAL

1 ______________________________

____

2 ______________________________

____

3 ______________________________

____

4 ______________________________

____

5 ______________________________

____

CHAPTER 13

Finding Your Niche Economy

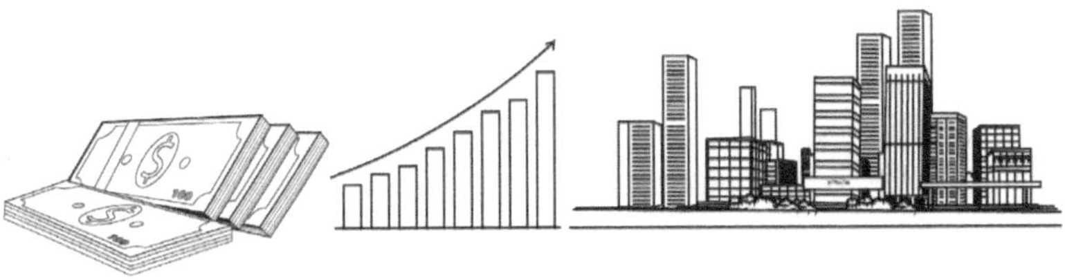

"You are the light of the world. A town built on a hill cannot be hidden. Neither do people light a lamp and put it under a bowl. Instead, they put it on its stand, and it gives light to everyone in the house" (Matthew 5:14-15)

We are the light of the world, not just the light of the church. We are to illuminate the cosmos. Each of us has a specific candle stand where we are to be positioned to give light to everyone in various places God put us. We are called to occupy till the Lord comes, and we need to discover the exact niche the Lord has called us to occupy for Him. Paul, while addressing the Corinthians said:

"I planted the seed, Apollos watered it, but God has been making it grow" (1 Corinthians 3:6 NIV).

Paul understood the importance and power of niche. He knew that there are different people with unique grace and gift to contribute their own quota to God's work, add value to God's people and to humanity in general. Paul identified himself as a planter, and Apollos as someone who waters. He might not be good at planting and watering at the same time. Not all founders of churches, organizations, and ministries are good at administrations. There is a need for people with specific gifts to come in to give their best for the development of God's Kingdom. The same applies to business, leadership and any other areas of life.

You cannot do everything. You could have many skills, gifts and abilities, but you cannot do everything. In fact, to be a master in what you do, you need to be a master at something. No one can be a master in everything. Masters are known for a specific thing. Mastery is gained overtime in doing specific things. If you attempt to do many things, you may end up doing nothing.

Focus is very important. Your focus should be well defined as a person. You should know why you are going into business, ministry or organization. Your focus is based on what your personal vision is and what your values are. Focus fixes your gaze, strength, energy, capacity and time on one thing. Focus helps you maximize yourself towards becoming better as a person and in what you do.

When it comes to finding your niche, the first thing to do is look inward. Your niche is first about you: Niche economy is not first about the business, but you. Your niche is about who you are before what you do. It is identifying your uniqueness before identifying the business you want to do. Whatever your business is, it is an outflow of your person. The functionality of your business depends on you. You are the first consideration when it comes to choosing a niche and building financial independence. Becoming a global leader and entrepreneur is not first about building financial prosperity through business.

The Bible says,

"For as he thinks in his heart, so is he..." (Proverbs 23:7)

Your mentality affects and influences what you do. The kind and quality of business you engage in are first about the kind and quality of thoughts that flow through your mind. Your person decides and determines the extent of the business. Before deciding the determinant of financial freedom, you need to work and develop yourself into a valuable personality.

The quality of your life will influence the value of your business. You must be able to add value to people's lives through your business. You should have something to offer people for money. What are you good at? What uniqueness do you have that can earn you people's attention and their wealth?

Many people do not know that our strengths are factored into what we can do. Some people are really good at managing relationships, and others do not know how to build and sustain relationships. As simple as this is, people make a fortune from relationship management either with individuals or organizations. Some people are good at giving valuable and wise counsel, and some others do not even know how to listen to people not to say counsel them.

Understand your personal vision

What is your vision? What are your life goals? What is your purpose? God can bless and multiply what He has given you. What specific assignment are you given? The uniqueness of your grace and gifts can also influence your niche. The Bible says,

> "Now there are distinctive varieties and distributions of endowments (gifts, extraordinary powers distinguishing certain Christians, due to the power of divine grace operating in their souls by the Holy Spirit) and they vary, but the [Holy] Spirit remains the same. And there are distinctive varieties of service and ministration, but it is the same Lord [Who is served]. And there are distinctive varieties of operation [of working to accomplish things], but it is the same God Who inspires and energizes them all in all. But to each one is given the manifestation of the [Holy] Spirit [the evidence, the spiritual illumination of the Spirit] for good and profit" (1 Corinthians 12:4-7 NIV).

You could be administrative or proactive, meticulous or creative, introvert or extrovert. Whatever your makeup is, your individual character can contribute to your niche. However, we need to balance this with the fact that God can stretch you to go beyond your limit so you can learn what seems totally out-of-box which can be useful for your life pursuits or business.

Understand your skills, gifts and talents

What do you know? What do you know better than others? What are you really good at? Your skills, gifts and talents are also important when considering your niche economy. Niche helps you narrow down your competition and give you a specific audience or market. Know your target and specific audience or market.

Niche research will help you identify your target market or audience out of the pool of possible audience or market. Many people are lost today, and many more are confused because they do too many things, and we do not know exactly what they do. You should be known for something, not many things.

Finally, you need to look outward. Identify your audience. What kinds of people do you want to reach? What are their characteristics? Jesus ministered to the poor and marginalized, Peter reached the Jews, while Paul focused on the Gentiles. Your business can target the elites, the middle class or the lower class. You can design a product that has a market that is limited to specific groups, or you target the masses with a product that can meet the needs of people. When you can identify your audience, you have successfully identified your audience or market. Since you now understand the needs of your audience or market, do not forget to offer values that are powered by vision and projected by excellence.

CHAPTER 14

Develop Your Brand And Tap Into Far Reaching Platforms

Go ye therefore, and teach all nations, baptizing them in the name of the Father, and of the Son, and of the Holy Ghost" (Mathew 20:19 KJV)

JESUS CHRIST ADMONISHED US to preach the Gospel to the world; churches and ministries need to spread the Gospel through the greatest worldwide communication tool, which is the Internet. In the days of the Bible, there was no social media, websites, or even the internet, yet the Gospel's message reached the world. Now that we have a platform to bring the world together, you need to leverage it to develop your brand and advance the Kingdom of God. With social media, you can engage an audience wider than your current location, farther than your imagination, and deeper than your knowledge.

A brand is the perception of people about you or your business; your brand is the uniqueness that distinguishes you from others. It covers your values, skills, talents, and knowledge. Your brand can be package and projected via a platform, which may be the pulpit, organizational meetings, conferences, social media, websites, or podcasts.

Developing a consistent brand can help people recognize your projected identity and message. Jesus provided a personal touch. He was visible and spoke to the people in a language that they understood through stories and parables. His brand personality stood out. He related to everyone, both young and old.

While you develop your brand, take your message to platforms where people are rather than expecting them to come to you or your websites. It takes value, packaging, and proper projection to engage the online community and convert a casual audience or readers to consistent readers and ardent followers.

Social media platforms such as Facebook and Instagram are very popular, and so are sites that allow people to broadcast messages, such as YouTube and Twitter. There are also online conferencing applications such as Zoom and Free Conference App. You must do good research on the right platform you want to use to get, engage, and manage your audience.

While you build your brand, you must balance your real identity and your projected personality. What you project yourself as must be consistent with who you are in Christ. Then, you must work on your motive. The challenge of digital platforms is the tendency to project us than it does to our message. But when we are sure that our focus is to get value and our message out there to reach out to lives to the glory of God, our hearts can be secured in God.

Then you need to know the exact thing you want to do online. This will influence your ministry or business activities, structure, operations, and functions that will be digitally inclined. You need to build a team of people who understand your vision, values, and identity to keep them on track on followers or audience engagement. Responsibility should be given to trained individuals who know what to do and how to get things done.

Create a structure to work it. Everything that works have a structure that makes it works. A structure gives guidelines to the plans, activities, and contents used to engage the audience. You also need to create brand rules that will engage your organizational or personal beliefs and core values.

Set markers and goals to help you monitor your strategy. You will need to monitor your search engine rankings, the contents that engage more people, and the increase in followership. While the motive is not the number, we also need to remember that the number of believers added to the church was monitored and recorded for us to read. So, we must ensure the platforms' objectives are being met, and the people are getting blessed by the content we place on those platforms. We must monitor the call to action for businesses and the effectiveness of the digital strategy we employ.

Also, to develop your brand, you must be a thought leader in your niche. You must develop brand integrity that people can trust with infallible resources. You must be willing to study people's culture in your field and dare to be different by being relevant and going counter-culture.

Finally, having an audience is not the same as engaging them. You can make your platforms more engaging by making your activities audience-oriented. Let them have the power to decide to an extent what happens on the platform to encourage engagement.

5 POINTS I HAVE LEARNED IN MY JOURNEY TO GOING GLOBAL

1 ______________________________

____

2 ______________________________

____

3 ______________________________

____

4 ______________________________

____

5 ______________________________

____

CHAPTER 15

Making Money And Making An Influence

How are money and influence interrelated? We all have a clue about making money. But it is not the same case with building influence. In society, influence and money are the basis of power. Power allows individuals to impact organizations, communities, and people around them. To fit into these places, you have to leave an impact. A job title or a senior position is not enough to sway people. Dorie Clark, the author of Entrepreneurial You, clarifies by saying, "The more you get done and progress with a project, the higher chances in getting a raise or promotion."

Nick Morgan, the author of Power Cues, adds that influencing others is a challenging task. At speed, the world is getting digitized; there is an information surplus. Innovations are bringing up an increased demand for results. It is easier to achieve them if you have backing. Power and money lie within the people. You only need to win their influence to enjoy them. Here are eleven useful guidelines to meet them.

Work Harder

No one hates to get successful, famous, and wealthy. People are doing extraordinary things to reach their dreams. Some are valid, while others are not. The sad part is a large number is hiding behind the umbrella, doing nothing significant. It is then motivating when you come across hardworking people. The feeling is much better when your work receives recognition. Working hard does not require someone always to watch over. It is critical to learn how to govern yourself. In those weird hours, when others are sleeping, get up to work. It is not easy, but it creates a superior impact. As you hunger for success, allow your body to rest to avoid burnout.

Do not Fear Risks

To stand out in the crowd, you have to paddle through the murky waters. Very few people are born into influential families. Most successful people have toiled harder to achieve it. The catch is that not everyone can take chances. People love simpler things in life. Taking risks requires putting your choices in the broader perspective of life. With that approach, you can realize that it is not rocket science to take a risk. By taking chances, you can do things that you only dreamt about. It opens up your mind to accomplish outrageous things. From taking a safari to forwarding that proposal, the risks will positively propel your life.

Practice Active Listening

Naturally, people enjoy sharing their thoughts. Sometimes, we get carried away and accumulate them. Sharing gives confirmation and a sense of wellbeing. For that reason, it is a great way to gain influence with others. To reciprocate, provide them with an ear too. Any person will regard you higher if you offer a shoulder to lean on. Always ask questions and show concern for the things they care about. Allowing people to open up to you is also therapeutic. It is even more accessible to introduce a business idea or product to people who have faith in you.

Approach Initiatives with Confidence

It is common for people to make biased judgments when you walk into a room. Those who walk in head high receive instant recognition. They have an easier time creating relationships. In most cases, they get prioritized when opportunities arise. No one would get comfortable to give a tender to someone stuttering with words.

In some cases, confidence is a symbol of power and capability. It requires plenty of self-love to gain poise and create an impact. In some cases, a first impression is the only chance given. If you mess up on it, you consider that deal done. On that note, feel the smile and posture when you walk through that door. The assurance in your voice speaks a volume. Displaying self-confidence is a crucial attribute in winning influence and power.

Start Small

As people grind on harder for success, they forget the simple things in life. There are those diminutive approaches that can change the definition of a relationship. If you want to stamp on your presence in a crowd, start with a smile. A smile breaks the ice as people get comfortable around you. Remember to keep track of people's names. It is human nature to feel at ease when people refer you by your name. Be courteous and offer help if required. Sometimes you may not manage to help, but it creates an impact if you listen. When introducing your product, do not start with exaggerated terms. Strive to be precise and clear. Your potential clients are looking for a solution, concentrate on that. Make sure always to follow up. Customers develop faith in you when they realize that you are thinking about them. Ideally, you depend on those clients for a living; learn how to keep them closer.

Practice Consistency

Your reputation comes first if you are looking for money, influence, and power. You will not manage to attract a lot of people if you keep on jumping through ideas. People also grow faith in individuals who keep their words. If you are not sure about something, do not give false information. Lying does last for long, soon people will find out. Influence is often associated with providing high-quality work. Focus on satisfying needs with unfailing attention. People will trust you more for your reliability. In the end, they will offer more promotion opportunities in the future.

Do not Run Away from Humor.

Life is not as complicated as we perceive. Sometimes a challenge can get solved through a humorous comment. Laughter breaks down barriers and creates positive relationships. After a long day, people will appreciate a relaxed approach. If you are funny naturally, take advantage of it. You can open up a blog or share your hilarious content on other platforms. Currently, humor is receiving a lot of attention. Comic individuals are minting money in the industry. Apart from appearing in stand up events, they are also hired as content developers. Remember that you do not require talent to keep people at ease. Find ways of making them jolly around you by choosing your words well. Always watch your body language and the tone of your voice. Keeping people comfortable goes a long way to creating wealth and power.

Build an Empire on Expertise

In the competitive world, people prefer a connection with a renowned expert. Getting that label does not happen overnight. Dorie adds by saying that expertise requires a reliable approach. Her advice is on immersing fully in the area of proficiency. You can do that by attending conferences or enrolling for that specialized certificate. When you graduate, do not keep your knowledge under wraps. Opening up a Facebook page or sharing on a blog is a splendid approach. These platforms allow you to market your products while sharing important information. The extra know-how empowers you to take headship positions in relevant organizations. Your primary plan here is to create an impact while making extra bucks. If you use the same enthusiasm in your new place, you will get a raise or promotion.

Satisfy People's Needs

You will have people on your side if you solve their problems. Do not take it for granted if someone approaches you for a solution. Nick advises on doing homework on how to help. Remember that people will give you undivided attention if they solve their issues. Personalize your solutions to cater to everyone. To create a more significant impact, look for solutions that benefit the whole community. If they ask for litter collection services, find ways to do so. In conversations, always use the term 'we' and not 'I.' This portrays you as a communal person and not self-centered.

Come up with Strategies

Promoting an idea requires strategic planning. You do not influence a group of people with thoughts all over the place. Dorie suggests creating a power map for guidance. To start with, you can come with a list of advisers on the issue at hand. Check if you can influence them directly or indirectly. Equip yourself with ample knowledge on how to approach these influential people. Keep in mind that you cannot penetrate the market without support from others. It would be best if you had people with similar ideologies at your back. If you are looking for monetary funding for a new product, give valid reasons. Do not exaggerate facts; sometimes, it keeps people away. Your supporters should not feel threatened by your plans. Instead, find credible ways to pull them over for a presence in the market.

Create Connections

In life, people embrace your idea or support you in business if they like you. Sometimes you may not have the best bread in town, but customers keep on streaming. The report created at the beginning translates the success story. Most flourishing businesses depend on referrals. A positive word of mouth leads to an extra dollar in the pocket. When you create great personal relationships, customers have faith in you. Selling is all about meeting their needs. If they receive exemplary services, they will come back and bring others.

5 POINTS I HAVE LEARNED IN MY JOURNEY TO GOING GLOBAL

1 ____________________

____

2 ____________________

____

3 ____________________

____

4 ____________________

____

5 ____________________

____

CHAPTER 16

Submit To Credible Leadership

As much as you have the knowledge, skill, and competence to demonstrate leadership, there is a need to submit to a credible leader. There are challenges that knowledge alone cannot overcome, and you would need the experience of a credible individual to help you through.

Sometimes, the key to our breakthrough in business, ministry, or finance may be in the hand of a leader. It was John the Baptist who announced and validated the ministry of Jesus. When you serve under a credible leadership, you will have access to his platform and audience, contributing to your growth as a leader.

Leadership is pivotal to growth. A leader does not just tell you to grow; he shows you the benefit of growing by his results while growing. No doubt, Jesus did not talk about leadership, but He showed us leadership. Leadership is not always in the talking but in action. Many people who project themselves to be leaders often lack the character and competence to express credible leadership.

Credibility is about trust. Credible Leadership is one that is based on trust, character, and result. Credibility makes people believe in leadership. Credible leadership is about the life of a leader. A credible leader models the character he desires to see and gets the results he wants to see in his followers, and contributes significantly to the follower's life.

As a leader and entrepreneur, the need for credible leadership cannot be underestimated. Even when it comes to biblical context, leaders are traced to their leaders. Elisha was a follower of Elijah. Timothy was led and mentored by Paul. Ruth followed Naomi.

It is quite sad that submission is only discussed in the subject of marriage. Submission is also important in leadership. Submission creates accountability. Apostle Paul wrote to the Corinthian Church,

> **"Follow my example, as I follow the example of Christ" (1 Corinthians 11:1 NIV).**

This implies, "submit to be as I submit to Christ." In other words, do not submit to a leader who does not have someone he submits to. Ultimately, we are to submit to the leadership of Christ.

We must submit to leadership so that we can learn how to serve. A good leader is one that is good at following. To become good leaders, we must submit as good followers to credible leadership. Submission means yielding to the guidance of another. It means letting go for the benefit of others.

Do not just submit to leadership; be specific in your choice. Submit to a specific area of need. Do not submit to leadership under a music minister when you need help with your business. Do not submit to leadership under a businessman when you know you are going into ministry.

Submit to someone who has excelled in a particular area of life you desire to develop. You can submit to a Godly business leader for guidance in your business. You can submit to a Godly couple to oversee you and your partner's journey through courtship. If you have a challenge with your personal walk with God through prayer and Bible study, you can submit to a pastor you honor and admire to guide you through.

While we am not proposing that you should not have someone you generally submit to, we suggest you also get specific leaders to help and guide you through specific areas of life. This is because leaders have their strengths, gifts, and graces, which are unique to them, and they also have their weaknesses. Specificity leads to specialization. You should prayerfully and willingly submit to a credible leader.

Iron sharpens iron

> **"As iron sharpens iron, so one person sharpens another." (Proverbs 27:17 NIV)**

When you submit to credible leadership, you become credible. As a leader, you will become better by the sharpening of another leader. Of course, God's Word is His comprehensive equipment for transforming lives, but He can also use those whom He has sharpened by His Word to sharpen us. It is only iron that can sharpen iron; it takes a credible leader to make another leader credible.

You can get your knowledge, skill, and experience sharpened by another. You can learn wisdom by following and learning from another. A credible leader can sharpen your skills, knowledge, and give you exposure. He can provide relevant resources needed for your growth and development. Submitting will offer you the opportunity to draw from the bank of knowledge of the leader you submit to.

Leaders are ladders. They can be the link between where you are and where you need to be. When you stand on your leaders' shoulders, you can see farther, better, and clearer. There are times you will learn from their wisdom gotten through good and bad experiences. Sometimes, it cost years to learn the wisdom you will learn in a few hours or days of interacting with them.

Credible leaders can stimulate your growth as a person and in your professional career, business, or ministry. They guide towards setting specific and realistic goals needed to ensure your development and success. They also help you monitor your growth.

Sometimes, things will get difficult, and you might be discouraged, but a credible leader will encourage and even offer you help along your journey. The fact that they are ahead of you is enough to drive you to keep going. The successes and the hurdles they surmounted are enough inspiration to drive you through your challenges and inspire your success.

Leaders can also discipline you. They can be harsh on you. This is not to make you feel bad, but to learn. The higher you go as a leader, the more demand for discipline. Discipline can sustain you in integrity and honesty.

5 POINTS I HAVE LEARNED IN MY JOURNEY TO GOING GLOBAL

1 ______________________________

____

2 ______________________________

____

3 ______________________________

____

4 ______________________________

____

5 ______________________________

____

CHAPTER 17

Networking With Other Leaders

NETWORKING IS THE PROCESS of meeting new people and interacting with them. Networking has a great value as it makes someone expand in their thinking and encounter new challenges and opportunities.

A good leader should not be a lone ranger but should be in a position to step out and get to meet new people, especially the people they share their interests with. The world we live in is a social world where every person will need the other at any given time, as no man is an Island.

Although different church denominations have got different missions and visions, they should not let that make them not come together to benefit from networking. This is because believers are united in Christ Jesus.

Different church denominations should be free to partner and network with each other for the sake of the gospel. Jesus Christ distributed various gifts to the church with the intention that through the church networking, they will come to the unity of faith and, in the long run, benefit one another.

> **"And He Himself gave some to be apostles, some prophets, some evangelists, and some pastors and teachers, for the equipping of the saints for the work of ministry, for the edifying of the body of Christ, *till we all come to the unity of the faith* and of the knowledge of the Son of God, to a perfect man, to the measure of the stature of the fullness of Christ;" (Ephesians 4:11-13).**

Every gift to the body of Christ is for the benefit of all. *"As each one has received a gift, minister it to one another, as good stewards of the manifold grace of God."* (1 Peter 4:10).

Benefits of Networking

Inspiration/ motivation.

When leaders meet and network, they inspire one another. The church in Jerusalem understood the benefits of this principle of Networking as one time they had to send Barnabas to the church in Antioch to meet with men who were leaders from Cyprus and

Cyrene. The results are clearly seen when Barnabas became an encouragement to them.

> "But some of them were men from Cyprus and Cyrene, who, when they had come to Antioch, spoke to the Hellenists, preaching the Lord Jesus. And the hand of the Lord was with them, and a great number believed and turned to the Lord. "Then news of these things came to the ears of the church in Jerusalem, and they sent out Barnabas to go as far as Antioch. When he came and had seen the grace of God, ***he was glad and encouraged them all that with purpose of heart; they should continue with the Lord.***" (Acts 11:20-23).

Access to opportunities.

Leaders who network are easily accessible to new opportunities than those who only work in their institution. This is because they get to meet new people and new challenges. Networking leaders can easily fulfill their mission and, at the same time, expand their ministry.

The Apostles of the early church had a great impact on their mission to spread the gospel as they coordinated in ministry. They were not selfish, but they could use one another and create new opportunities to spread the gospel.

> "Then it pleased the apostles and elders, with the whole church, to send chosen men of their own company to Antioch with Paul and Barnabas, namely, Judas who was also named Barsabbas, and Silas, leading men among the brethren." (Acts 15:22).

1. *Creates a positive influence*
   When leaders come together through networking, they exchange a lot. This is because the people that you will hang around with have a major role in influencing you. During networking, everyone gets challenged on seeing how other leaders run their affairs, and they will desire to implement what they had seen working somewhere.

King Solomon knew this fact very well when he wrote that *"As iron sharpens iron, So a man sharpens the countenance of his friend."* (Proverbs 27:17).

2. *Increases confidence*
   As leaders network, they develop confidence as they meet new people every time they interact during networking. Confident in ministry is one of the key elements, especially for a leader. A confident leader can lead people without fear. Communication skills are improved with confidence. This will, in turn, improve the process of delivering a particular message and more so if it is the teaching of the word of God.

3. *Creates friendship*
   Most leaders create new friends through networking. A good leader is the one who is ready to create friendships because it increases someone's network. By doing this, the leader will be able to reach more people at the same time and make an impact on their ministry.

When Jesus Christ decided to pass through Samaria as recorded in John's gospel, He met the Samaritan woman at the well.

Although, at first, the Samaritan woman was not willing to talk to Jesus, after realizing that He was the Messiah, she had no option but to invite Jesus Christ to her people.

It started from Jesus Christ meeting one woman to Him witnessing to the entire city, and the end result is that many believed.

> "And many of the Samaritans of that city believed in Him because of the word of the woman who testified, He told me all that I ever did. So when the Samaritans had come to Him, they urged Him to stay with them; ***and He stayed there two days. And many more believed because of His own word.*** Then they said to the woman, Now we believe, not because of what you said, for we ourselves have heard Him and we know that this is indeed the Christ, the Savior of the world." (John 4:39-42).

Acquisition of new information.

When leaders meet, they share ideas and acquire new information. This means that they will gain information and acquire new skills that will help them in leadership.

When the queen of Sheba heard of King Solomon's wisdom, she knew as a leader, she needed to learn something from King Solomon. So she set on a journey to meet King Solomon.

> "Now when the queen of Sheba heard of the fame of Solomon concerning the name of the Lord, she came to test him with hard questions. She came to Jerusalem with a very great retinue, with camels that bore spices, very much gold, and precious stones; and when she came to Solomon, she spoke with him about all that was in her

heart. "So Solomon answered all her questions; there was nothing so difficult for the king that he could not explain it to her. And when the queen of Sheba had seen all the wisdom of Solomon, the house that he had built, the food on his table, the seating of his servants, the service of his waiters and their apparel, his cupbearers, and his entryway by which he went up to the house of the Lord, there was no more spirit in her. Then she said to the king: It was a true report which I heard in my own land about your words and your wisdom. "However, I did not believe the words until I came and saw with my own eyes; and indeed, the half was not told me. Your wisdom and prosperity exceed the fame of which I heard." (1 Kings 10:1-7)

Accountability

When leaders form networks, they form various activities that will bring them together; it may be grouped for Bible discussion or investment groups. This will make the leaders try as much as possible to be accountable to each other in terms of availability and other aspects like finances.

When this happens, the leaders should be more careful when carrying out their responsibilities compared to when they only have ministerial isolation responsibilities.

Finally, the entire Great Commission of Jesus Christ to spread the gospel to all corners of the world is rooted in the ability to effectively network with leaders and people all over the world.

When Apostle Paul was to defend the gospel in Rome, he had to call the leaders to reason with them.

"***And it came to pass after three days that Paul called the leaders of the Jews together.*** So when they had come together, he said to them:

Men and brethren, though I have done nothing against our people or the customs of our fathers, yet I was delivered as a prisoner from Jerusalem into the hands of the Romans, who, when they had examined me, wanted to let me go because there was no cause for putting me to death. "But when the Jews spoke against it, I was compelled to appeal to Caesar, not that I had anything of which to accuse my nation. For this reason, therefore, I have called for you, to see you and speak with you, because for the hope of Israel, I am bound with this chain. "Then they said to him, "We neither received letters from Judea concerning you nor have any of the brethren who came reported or spoken any evil of you. "But we desire to hear from you what you think; for concerning this sect, we know that it is spoken against everywhere." (Acts 28:17-22)

5 POINTS I HAVE LEARNED IN MY JOURNEY TO GOING GLOBAL

1 ____

2 ____

3 ____

4 ____

5 ____

CHAPTER 18

Have A Mindset Of 1000 Times More Blessings

"For as he thinks in his heart, so is he..." (Proverbs 23:7 AMP)

ONE OF THE MOST powerful things God gave to man is the mind. The mind is the seat of will, intellect, and emotions. All that you will ever achieve will first pass through your mind before it enters your life. Your life within creates your life without. The quality of your mindset is very important to the quality of your life.

A mindset for a thousand times more blessings focuses on boundless possibilities and limitless opportunities available in business, life, and any other means of accessed blessings. Such a mindset is optimistic and is not moved by the things seen (present), but sees the unseen, and with faith, creates the desired scene (future). The mind is so powerful that the Bible says,

"For as he thinks in his heart, so is he..." (Proverbs 23:7 AMP)

You are the exact physical expression and representation of your thought. Abundance starts with developing a mindset for it. Until you have the mindset for abundance, it cannot materialize in your life. The extent of your blessing is not dependent on God but on you. You determine the container to receive God's blessing. God has said He would open the windows of heaven to pour out His blessing. What determines what you get is the volume of your container!

Do you remember the story of Elisha and one of the sons of the prophets?

> **"The wife of a man from the company of the prophets cried out to Elisha, "Your servant my husband is dead, and you know that he revered the Lord. But now his creditor is coming to take my two boys as his slaves." Elisha replied her, "How can I help you? Tell me, what do you have in your house?" "Your servant has nothing there at all," she said, "except a small jar of olive oil." Elisha said, "Go around and ask all your neighbors for empty jars. Don't ask for just a few.**

> Then go inside and shut the door behind you and your sons. Pour oil into all the jars, and as each is filled, put it to one side." She left him and shut the door behind her and her sons. They brought the jars to her and she kept pouring. When all the jars were full, she said to her son, "Bring me another one." But he replied, "There is not a jar left." Then the oil stopped flowing." (2 Kings 4:1-6 NIV).

You must have enough vessels to receive God's abundance for you. There more the vessels, the more it flows. The blessings of God are limitless and boundless and will not take the shape of our mindset. The more the ideas, businesses, platforms, and initiatives, God's blessing will keep flowing. We limit God when we do not have more vessels through which we can receive His abundance.

Amazingly, the oil that filled several vessels was once contained in a single jar. The oil has potentials but was limited by the size of the container. This is the same with God's blessing. Your current level of blessing is not because of God's promises, power, or potential for multiplication, but your mindset to receive. Even if it is to borrow more vessels or invest in others, your mindset to receive must be enlarged to a thousand times to receive a thousand times blessing.

How to develop a mindset for a thousand times blessing?

You can make a transition by renewing your mind by learning God's Word's wisdom towards abundance. The Bible says,

> "Do not conform to the pattern of this world, but be transformed by the renewing of your mind. Then you will be able to test and

approve what God's will is – his good, pleasing and perfect will." (Romans 12:2).

Do not develop the mindset of the world, nor learn their disposition to prosperity. There is a unique pattern by which we access and receive God's blessing that is quite different from the mindset of those in the world. God's good, pleasing, and perfect will is that you have abundance, and you can access this by shaping your mindset towards receiving.

The Bible says,

"Beloved, I pray that you may prosper in every way and [that your body] may keep well, even as [I know] your soul keeps well and prosper." (3 John 1:2).

God's will for you is to prosper in every way. You should get rid of the mindset that assumes it is not God's will to bless and prosper you. When you study God's Word, you will realize people like Abraham, David, Solomon, and even Joseph of Arimathaea (the rich disciple, Matthew 27:57) were blessed with abundance. The Word of God gives you light, renews your mind, starves your fear, shapes your thinking, and positions you to receive an abundance mindset. You will come to realize that God is the source of your blessing, the abundant source for everything blessing you can think of.

The Bible says,

"And my God will meet all your needs according to the riches of his glory in Christ Jesus." (Philippians 4:19 NIV).

According to your deservedness, God will not bless you, but according to the riches of His glory in Christ. HHiHHHasdHis blessing is not based on you but according to Him. The Lord can open the windows of heaven to pour blessings on you, but you also need to open the windows of your mind to receive abundance. To bless others, you must keep an open mind. An old adage that says, *"When God enlarges and bless you more, build a bigger table, not a higher fence."* The tendency to hoard God's blessing may come upon you, but you must not align with such a mindset. God blesses you to bless others. Let me share a parable that Jesus told His disciples:

> **"And he told them a parable, saying, "The land of a rich man produced plentifully, and he thought to himself, 'what shall I do, for I have nowhere to store my crops?' And he said, 'I will do this: I will tear down my barns and build larger ones, and there I will store all my grains and my goods. And I will say to my soul, "Soul, you have ample goods laid up for many years; relax, eat, drink and be merry." But God said to him, 'Fool! This night your soul is required of you, and the things you have prepared, whose will they be?" (Luke 12:16-20 ESV).**

When the mind is not renewed to honor the Lord with our possessions, there will be trouble. When God's blessing flows into your life, you must open your life so the blessing can flow into the lives of others. When there was no vessel to pour into, the oil ceased. When blessing doesn't flow out of you, it will make you saturated in a way that inhibits God's fresh blessings from flowing into your life the more. As you develop an abundance mindset, you also need to develop a giving or benevolent mindset.

5 POINTS I HAVE LEARNED IN MY JOURNEY TO GOING GLOBAL

1 ______________________________

____

2 ______________________________

____

3 ______________________________

____

4 ______________________________

____

5 ______________________________

____

CHAPTER 19

Avoid Spiritual Pride

THE FIRST AND WORST cause of errors that abound in our day and age is spiritual pride. This is the main door through which the devil comes into the hearts of those who are zealous for the advancement of Christ. Spiritual pride is one of the most harmful sins to your faith. It causes you to look away from Jesus and shines a spotlight on you. By spiritual pride, the mind defends itself against errors and defends itself against light by which it might be corrected and reclaimed.

The spiritually proud man thinks he is full of light already and feels that he does not need instruction, so he is ready to ignore the offer of it. One under the influence of spiritual pride is more apt to instruct others than to inquire about his personal need for instruction. The eminently humble Christian thinks he needs help from everybody, but he that is spiritually proud thinks everybody needs his help.

Spiritual pride is an insidious enemy that we all continually must guard against and fight. It was one of the main sins of the Pharisees. They thought they were a notch above their fellow Jews (John 9:28-34) and far above the despised Gentile dogs. To confront such pride, Jesus told the parable of the Pharisee and the publican who went up to the temple to pray (Luke 18:9-14).

> **"To some who were confident of their own righteousness and looked down on everyone else, Jesus told this parable: "Two men went up to the temple to pray, one a Pharisee and the other a tax collector. The Pharisee stood by himself and prayed: 'God, I thank you that I am not like other people- robbers, evildoers, adulterers – or even like this tax collector. I fast twice a week and give a tenth of all I get.' "But the tax collector, [merely] standing at a distance, would not even look up to heaven, but beat his breast and said, 'God, have mercy on me, a sinner.' "I tell you that this man, rather than the other, went home justified before God. For all in those who exalt themselves will be humbled, and those who humble themselves will be exalted."**

The Pharisee thanked God that he wasn't like the publican. But how many times have you read that story and thought, "Thank God that I'm not like that Pharisee!"? Jesus condemns the Pharisees for saying one thing and doing another and doing everything they do just for how it looks to other people. The Pharisees loved the attention and the respect they received for their position, but they had no desire to genuinely help other people or love God.

Another indicator that you are trapped in spiritual pride is envying other people's spiritual gifts. Pride is the reason we do so little good for others with our gifts. When pride prevails, we pray, preach, comfort, or console to be thought good by others, rather than do good to others. We set ourselves upon a spiritual pedestal and, in a manner of speaking, except those we serve to worship at the shrine of our good works. Will God honor such efforts? He has told us in no uncertain terms that He will not share His glory with anyone else (Isaiah 48:11).

The humble man may have Satan at his right hand to oppose him, but the proud man will find himself in a worse fix. God Himself will be there to resist him. If you doubt it, read His Word:

> **"[He] resists the proud, but gives grace unto the humble." (James 4:6).**

Apostle Peter had this besetting danger of spiritual pride in mind when he wrote to the Church:

> **"Humble yourselves therefore under the mighty hand of God, that He may exalt you in due time." (1 Peter 5:6).**

"Whosoever exalts himself shall be abased, and he that shall humble himself shall be exalted," said the Master.

When you feel your attendance at meetings, reading of so many pages of scriptures per day, distribution of so many tracts or circulation, or loaning of so many books are matters to be boasted of, then take care! When one hears no proper answer except his own, any of the questions should be considered dangerous spiritual pride symptoms.

> **"Pride goes before destruction, and a haughty spirit before a fall." (Proverbs 16:18 AMP)**

Consider King Nebuchadnezzar. At the height of his pride, God took him down and turned him into a wild beast for 7 years. We must be diligent to guard against pride in our lives as believers. Christians are not exempt from the sin of pride, and we can be seduced into it by success, even success that comes from serving the LORD. King Uzziah was a young king who started by following the LORD, yet when he was strong and successful, he succumbed to pride, and the LORD struck him with leprosy.

Peter is known for having a big mouth and putting his foot in it a lot. He often says things on a whim and out of pride. In this example, he tells Jesus that he would never fall away from Him even if others fall away. But when others abandoned Jesus at his trial, Peter also abandoned Him (Matthew 26:33-35).

Pride makes us think that we will always do the right thing. There is a big difference between thinking; we will always do the right thing and having the wisdom to know that we are always capable of doing the wrong thing and then choosing to do the right thing.

But how shall we safeguard ourselves against this spiritual pride, knowing as we do its insidious character and evil influence? How may we know that we are keeping ourselves in the love of God and not stray away toward spiritual pride?

1. Pray for humility. When we ask God for characteristics like humility, He answers by giving us opportunities to be humble. You won't just wake up one day without the urge to compare yourself to others, but you will learn to celebrate others' lives without jealousy.

2. Remember that salvation is by grace alone. Spiritual pride creeps in when we forget that salvation is by grace alone, not because of anything good in us. God is in charge of salvation. He is working according to His sovereign, gracious choice. No one, whether Jew or Gentile, deserves salvation. It is always by God's grace alone. Ephesians 2:8-9 says,

> **"For by grace, you have been saved through faith; and that not of yourselves, it is the gift of God; not as a result of works, so that no one may boast."**

3. Submission and servant-hood are safeguards for pride. We need to submit to God daily. We need to humble ourselves under His mighty hand. We must understand that it's with/through Him that all things are made possible. All the glory belongs to Him. Submit to His Will and Way. Stop focusing on "I" and focus on Jesus! Humble yourself before God has to humble you (Isaiah 2:11). Less of me and more of You, God! Then start serving others. Great leaders serve! Get the focus away from yourself and off of what others can do for you. See what you can do to be a blessing to someone. Submission and servant-hood are all traits of the

humbled. Humbled people know they aren't better than anyone else and that they're only here by the grace of God. Humbled people don't exalt themselves; they exalt the Lord.

4. We must imitate the One Who is the perfect model of humility, Jesus Christ, the Son of God; Jesus, Who said, *"Blessed are the poor in spirit, for theirs is the kingdom of heaven."* (Matt. 5:3); Jesus, Who humbled Himself to share in our humanity; Jesus, Who taught His disciples to take the lowest place, who washed the feet of the Apostles, who came to serve and not to be served, and who said, *"Take my yoke upon you, and learn from me; for I am gentle and lowly in heart."* (Matt. 11:29).

Allow Jesus to undo the knots spiritual pride has created in your heart. You are not better than others to Him. You are not perfect. You are not meant to be the center of your story. Humbly and graciously allow God to undo your pride. Jesus did not consider Himself too spiritually great to help us. He is love. And we can be less prideful and more loving every day if we allow Him to work in our hearts.

5 POINTS I HAVE LEARNED IN MY JOURNEY TO GOING GLOBAL

1 ______________________________

____

2 ______________________________

____

3 ______________________________

____

4 ______________________________

____

5 ______________________________

____

CHAPTER 20

Position To Be People's Mentor

"He appointed twelve that they might be with him and that he might send them out to preach." (Mark 3:14 NIV).

Relationships are God's means of blessing us, and mentorship is one of such relationships. Jesus showed us an example of mentorship. He appointed twelve to be with Him. In other words, they are to interact and learn of and from Him. Jesus could not be everywhere simultaneously, so He mentored twelve people, who in the process became transformed so much that they could replicate His results and also express His character and excellence. Although the transformation of people is God's responsibility through the Holy Spirit and God's Word, He uses those who have been trained as an instrument to train others. The Bible says,

> **"Now I commit you to God and to the word of his grace, which can build you up and give you an inheritance among all those who are sanctified." (Acts 20:32 NIV).**

Often, God uses people whom He can entrust the life and destiny of His upcoming instruments (the younger ones) to skillful use the word and also encourage discipline and accountability for their proper growth and development.

Mentoring is essential as a Christian leader. It shows the effectiveness of your influence and the ability to replicate your success through another person in a quicker, better, greater, and more effective way with the wisdom you have embodied over the years. In fact, positioning to be a mentor to others creates a consciousness of your life and character because they greatly influence the people you lead or mentor.

Mentoring is not a new concept. It dates back to the Old Testament. Although the word mentor or mentorship did not appear in the Bible, there were situations and interactions where a wiser, older, or more experienced person guides and leads another individual in different aspects of life. In Exodus 18, Moses Father-in-law, Jethro, observed his leadership style and suggested a strategy to manage the situation more effectively. The experience of a mentor is a pearl for the mentee.

Also, in the book of Deuteronomy, Moses mentored Joshua, who eventually became His successor. The Disciples of Christ also became His successors. You mustn't wait till you are about to leave the earth to mentor your successor. Mentorship is important to birthing an effective successor. In the New Testament, it is referred to as Discipleship.

Expanding Influence

As a leader with Christ as Lord, you have the advantage to make use of Kingdom principles to unleash and maximize people's potentials. The more you mentor people, the greater your influence will become mentors to others, while you become an exemplary mentor. For anyone you mentor, you have successfully created a tributary to reach out to those connected to them.

Mentoring expands your influence and also helps preserve it. It allows you to be entrusted with people and entrust them with wisdom and working principles. It also serves as an opportunity to also transfer the knowledge of God to them. You will teach them through your life and what God has done in and for you.

Mentorship Engagement

There are certain things you need to know and practice as you position to be a mentor; they are as follows:

- **Listen:** One of the most important things you will need to practice is listening. You might be tempted to teach always, but be a listener if you want to be effective. Many times, the problem or challenge they are having will surface while they talk to you. You must be willing to listen so that you can know your mentee's perspective and get into their heart.

- **Pray:** As a Christian mentor, you are an intercessor. When you listen to your mentee, and understand the specific needs, take the matter to God in prayer. When you pray for them, you strengthen the spiritual bond you have with the person.
- **Expose:** One of the advantages you have as a Mentor is that you have more experiences and exposure than they do. You are to teach, train, and trust them with responsibility so that they can get better. They will need you to give them a platform to develop their uniqueness, build their strength, and evaluate their competence. You also need to expose them to other competent individuals in areas where you are not, so they become balanced in their learning.
- **Model:** The most effective way to teach something is to model it. As a mentor, you must be conscious that your character and actions speak more than your words. The people you mentor will listen to you, but they will do what you do. You should set the pace in every area of your life so that you can be seen as an example.
- **Teach:** Jesus took advantage of almost every situation to teach the disciples something new. Mentorship demands resourcefulness. You cannot know everything, but you should have enough knowledge to keep the people you mentor inspired, guided, and helped.
- **Ask questions:** Questioning helps create light to a matter or situation. When you ask practical questions, your mentee will be exposed to deep and critical thinking. Also, it aids

feedbacks on the effectiveness of your mentorship relationship with them.

How do you get people to mentor?

As you grow through life, your life, light, and success will attract people. A character of light is influence; it draws people closer to you. At the beginning of Jesus' ministry, after He was baptized, John the Baptist told his followers to follow Jesus, the Lamb of God. Your results in life can command followership from far and wide.

You can engage your audience physically and via social media. Social media has made interaction, communication, and followership engagement easier. When people realize you are a man of value, the next thing they want to do is follow you on social media.

You can also look out for young people who are in your field, who needs guidance. When you help them out in their difficulty, they automatically become accountable to you because of your input in their lives. God's expectation over you is that you multiply. This is not about giving birth to many children, but giving birth to many lives that can reproduce the seed of God, the seed of excellence, and the seed of grace at work in your life.

5 POINTS I HAVE LEARNED IN MY JOURNEY TO GOING GLOBAL

1 ______________________________

2 ______________________________

3 ______________________________

4 ______________________________

5 ______________________________

CHAPTER 21

Mentoring Other Leaders

EFFECTIVE LEADERSHIP HAS MENTORSHIP. Leaders should realize that they will not always be in leadership positions, so they should have mentoring other leaders.

Some of the greatest examples in the Bible of leaders who mentored others are Elijah and Elisha, Jesus Christ and His disciples, and Apostle Paul with his son Timothy.

For mentorship to be effective, first, there must be a good relationship between the mentor and the mentee. So the first step a mentor should take is to create and develop a friendship.

A good mentor has the following qualities:

They set a good example as a role model.

A mentor should lead by example, as their mentees always look upon them in every aspect. Any misconduct done by the mentor can affect the mentee's trust in the mentor and the relationship.

When Apostle Paul is instructing his son to lead as a good example to the other believers, he knew very well that he was preparing Timothy for leadership. Many will be looking upon him in doctrine and character.

> **"Let no one despise your youth, but be an example to the believers in word, in conduct, in love, in spirit, in faith, in purity." (1 Timothy 4:12)**

Sharing experience with the mentee.

Good mentors are willing to share their experiences with the people they are leading. This is because the mentees learn better if they are given practical experience from their mentors.

Apostle Paul not only shared the gospel with his son Timothy but also his life experience. *"But you must continue in the things which you have learned and been assured of,* ***knowing from whom you have learned them."*** **(**2 Timothy 3:14)

Good mentors care about the next generation.

Mentors have a place for the next generation at heart. They are very eager to correct any error before it is passed to the next generations. During the era of Moses's law, parents being the mentors of their children were instructed to teach (pass down) everything they had heard to their children and grandchildren. This is the spirit that a mentor should have.

"Only take heed to yourself, and diligently keep yourself, lest you forget the things your eyes have seen, and lest they depart from your heart all the days of your life. ***And teach them to your children and your grandchildren.***" (Deuteronomy 4:9)

Provide positive feedback.

Mentors should be very careful about how they provide feedback on the learning process. Any negative feedback can affect the relationship that the mentee had with their mentor, which can, in turn, affect the entire response to the mentorship program.

The feedback given should be open and true and not exaggerated. Look at the examples of feedbacks that Apostle Paul wrote to the churches in Ephesus and Thessalonica.

"Therefore I also, after I heard of your faith in the Lord Jesus and your love for all the saints, do not cease to give thanks for you, making mention of you in my prayers." (Ephesians 1: 15-16)

"For from you, the word of the Lord has sounded forth, not only in Macedonia and Achaia but also in every place. ***Your faith toward God has gone out so that we do not need to say anything.***" (1 Thessalonians 1:8).

Are enthusiastic.

Mentors should be excited and self-motivated. They should not be struggling to mentor, but mentorship should come from their hearts. Mentors should not be struggling with doing their work but instead, enjoy it.

Apostle Paul was excited about the church in Corinth, although they still had their struggles in Christianity and serving God.

> **"Therefore I rejoice that I have confidence in you in everything." (2 Corinthians 7:16).**

Encourages someone to step out of their comfort zone.

Mentors should be in a position to realize that those they are mentoring have stayed long in their comfort zone. They should encourage their mentee to break camp and scale for greater heights. By doing this, they would desire their mentees to grow.

Apostle Paul encourages Timothy like this; "*Therefore I remind you to stir up the gift of God, which is in you through the laying on of my hands. For God has not given us a spirit of fear, but of power and of love and of a sound mind.*" (2 Timothy 1:6-7)

Mentors are active listeners.

A mentor should be ready to listen attentively when the mentor is speaking. They should not be so busy to a point where they are not listening to what the mentee is saying.

They should be experts in their field.

A good mentor should be well conversant with what he intends to impart in the mentee. Apostle Paul encourages Timothy to continue with the doctrine as it will save him and the people that hear him teaching. This means that Apostle Paul wanted Timothy to increase in knowledge in what he was teaching others.

"Meditate on these things; give yourself entirely to them, that your progress may be evident to all. Take heed to yourself and to the doctrine. Continue in them, for in doing this, you will save both yourself and those who hear you." (1 Timothy 4:15-16).

CHALLENGES IN MENTORING RELATIONSHIPS

For a mentorship program to run smoothly, both parties must be reading from the same page as they are mutual partners in this program. These are some of the challenges in the mentoring program.

Unrealistic expectations.

This applies on both sides, that is, from the side of the mentor or mentee. The mentor can sometimes overload the mentee with too much work expecting them to finish. He may also expect an instant change in the character of the mentee.

Therefore there should be proper goal setting. The goals set in any mentorship program should be SMART. This means that they should be Specific, Measurable, Achievable, Realistic, and Time-bound.

This may require a lot of patience from both sides as it should be known as growth and change takes time. *"And a servant of the Lord must not quarrel but* ***be gentle to all, able to teach, patient."*** (2 Timothy 2:24).

Meeting as scheduled

The date, time, and duration of the meetings should be adhered to. If there is any change in the day or time of the meeting, it should be communicated earlier; this is because the parties involved may be having a busy daily routine that need not be interfered with. If this issue of time is not well addressed, it may affect the whole program as no party would tolerate wasting their time waiting for the other party.

There should be proper time management put in place so as not to affect any party. Meetings should be planned earlier and dates set aside. The scheduled duration of the meetings should not be underestimated.

Lack of commitment in either of the two parties.

If the mentee seems to be lacking commitment in the program, the mentor should work out to find what might be the cause of the lack of commitment. Maybe the mentor-mentee relationship may not be working well, or the mentee has found out that the two don't share the same interests.

If the root cause of lack of commitment is addressed earlier, it can prevent them from wasting time and resources on a program that seems not to be working.

Lack of motivation.

Mentors in any mentorship program need to be motivated. Motivated individuals work more efficiently. The mentee should try in all means to make sure that the mentor is well motivated. This can be done by appraisal or making sure that the mentor gets the necessary materials that he may need in time.

The church should realize that mentoring other leaders are one of the crucial things that God is involved in. So there should be constant prayer and a lot of patience practiced. Both the mentor and mentee should commit themselves to God by prayer, knowing that God is working in us for the sake of transforming us. The word of God, which is the mirror, should also be emphasized in the entire program.

> "But we all, with unveiled face, beholding as in a mirror the glory of the Lord, are being transformed into the same image from glory to glory, just as by the Spirit of the Lord." (2 Corinthians 3:18).

5 POINTS I HAVE LEARNED IN MY JOURNEY TO GOING GLOBAL

1 ____

2 ____

3 ____

4 ____

5 ____

CHAPTER 22

Teaching Leaders

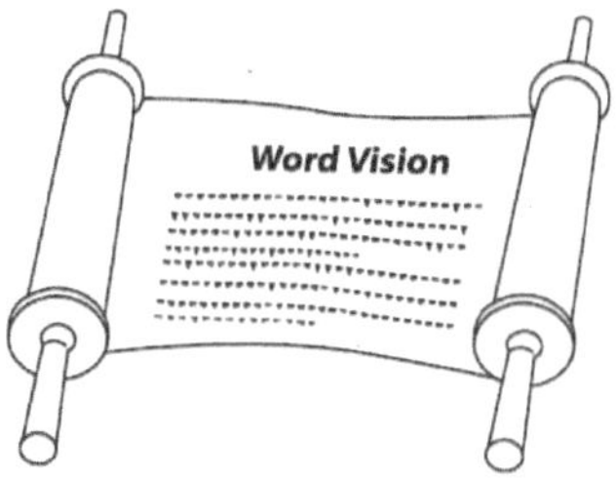

"Teaching them to observe all things that I have commanded you; **and lo, I am with you always, even to the end of the age." Amen. (Mathew 28:20).**

THESE WERE THE LAST words of Jesus Christ, which are also known as the *Great Commission.* Jesus Christ knew very well that there must be the passing of knowledge from one person to the other for His ministry to go on. Therefore, he had to invest a lot in His disciples before leaving them behind to continue with His ministry.

This is the power of equipping and teaching leaders. It assures continuity of a ministry even if the leader or founder is long gone. Apostle Paul instructs Timothy like this; *"And the things that you have heard from me among many witnesses, commit these* ***to faithful men who will be able to teach others also.***" (Timothy 2:2).

Apostle Paul is much concerned about the qualifications or qualities of leaders that should be entrusted with the gospel. Here are some of the most important qualities that a mentee should possess.

Faithfulness.

This is the act of being relied on. It is also one of the fruits of the Holy Spirit. Without faithfulness, no matter how a leader may be equipped, he cannot pass information or exhibit good leadership skills. Apostle Paul reminds the church of Corinth of this fact.

> "Let a man so consider us, as servants of Christ and stewards of the mysteries of God. ***Moreover, it is required in stewards that one be found faithful.***" (1 Corinthians 4:1-2).

When a leader is faithful, he can carry out his function without being supervised. He will carry out his duty wholeheartedly without complaining or grumbling because he realizes that he is not working for men but God.

> "Do all things without complaining and disputing," (Philippians 2:14).

> "And whatever you do, do it heartily, as to the Lord and not to men, knowing that from the Lord, you will receive the reward of the inheritance; for you serve the Lord Christ." (Colossians 3:23-24)

Availability

One who is to be taught should always be readily available. The disciples of Jesus Christ could follow Him whenever He went, be it during the day or the night. They had to drop their occupations and commitment to follow and learn from Jesus Christ. This calls for sacrifice.

This also goes hand in hand with time management. Anyone who wants to be taught must know how to manage time. Must always be available whenever they are needed to be taught.

King Solomon, the wisest human being, discovered one thing; that knowledge is the best thing that a man can desire to have.

> **"Also, *it is not good for a soul to be without knowledge*, And he sins who hastens with his feet." (Proverbs 19:2).**

Humility.

This is the act of being humble. A good leader should show a good example by being humble in all aspects. Being proud or rude will only result in someone not achieving their intended purpose.

Jesus Christ showed the highest form of humility by accepting to be sent to the world by His Father.

> **"Let this mind be in you which was also in Christ Jesus, who, being in the form of God, did not consider it robbery to be equal with God, but made Himself of no reputation, taking the form of a bondservant, and coming in the likeness of men. "And being found in appearance as a man, He humbled Himself and became obedient to the point of death, even the death of the cross." (Philippians 2:5 -7).**

Sacrifice and selflessness.

Sacrifice is one of the greatest virtue that is required in leadership. Anyone who wants to be taught should be ready to sacrifice his or her energy, time, and resources. This portrays a sense of selflessness.

As our good example of a leader, Jesus Christ was not forced to die on the cross. He was much willing to carry out His purpose. Look at what He told His disciples. "*Therefore, My Father loves Me* ***because I lay down My life that I may take it again.*** *No one takes it from Me, but I lay it down of Myself. I have the power to lay it down, and I have power to take it again. This command I have received from My Father.*" (John 10: 17-18).

A good leader should be willing to sacrifice all that he has for his course.

Not easily influenced by the world.

The love of the world is the major distractor of effective leadership. One cannot serve the world and, at the same time, serve God. The Bible says that you cannot serve two masters. You will either love one or hate someone. So you are either serving God or the world. It is a personal choice to make without being pushed.

Apostle Paul tried to mentor some of his disciples in preparation for the ministry, but some of them loved the world more than the ministry. By doing this, they failed.

> **"For Demas has forsaken me, having loved this present world, and has departed for Thessalonica—Crescens for Galatia, Titus for Dalmatia." (2 Timothy 4:10).**

Leaders are compared to soldiers getting instructions not from the world but from their Commander

> **"No one engaged in warfare entangles himself with the affairs of this life that he may please him who enlisted him as a soldier." (2 Timothy 2:4).**

IMPORTANCE OF TEACHING AND EQUIPPING LEADERS.

The parable of the talents taught by Jesus Christ in the book of Mathew chapter twenty-five shows how a leader can use what has been invested to bring out results. From the parable, we see the effectiveness of every leader.

One servant was given 5 talents, another 2, and another 1. The first two did their best and multiplied their talents, except the third, he hid his talent in the ground; therefore, he didn't utilize what was invested in him by his Lord.

This means that teaching leaders don't end in the class, but it should produce individual results. From the example of the first two servants, we can derive the importance of teaching leaders.

For effectiveness in handling the word of God

Leaders who have undergone training are usually effective in leadership. God is well pleased with effective leaders because they will carry out their duties with excellence. Jesus Christ told His disciples like this; *"A disciple is not above his teacher, but everyone who is perfectly trained will be like his teacher."* (Luke 6:40).

Apostle Paul instructs his son Timothy on the importance of God's word in equipping him for ministry.

"All Scripture is given by inspiration of God and is profitable for doctrine, for reproof, for correction, for instruction in righteousness that ***the man of God may be complete, thoroughly equipped for every good work."*** (2 Timothy 3:16-17).

"Study and be eager and do your utmost to present yourself to God approved (tested by trial), a workman who has no cause to be ashamed, ***correctly analyzing and accurately dividing [rightly handling and skillfully teaching] the Word of Truth."*** (2 Timothy 2:15 AMP).

To develop great stewardship

Teaching leaders is beneficial to both the one teaching and those who are being taught.

"If you lay all these instructions before the brethren, you will be a worthy steward and a good minister of Christ Jesus, ever nourishing your own self on the truths of the faith and of the good [Christian] instruction which you have closely followed." (1 Timothy 4:6AMP.)

"Take heed to yourself and to the doctrine. Continue in them, for in doing this, you will save both yourself and those who hear you." (1 Timothy 4:16)

For effective ministry work

Leaders who have passed through thorough teachings and training on leadership produce an effective result. This, in return, causes quick growth of a ministry as everyone knows what they are supposed to do, and they do it with ease and perfection.

When Apostle Paul got converted on his way to Damascus, he was first taken to Arabia, where he stayed for 3 years and was prepared by God for ministry. A leader should realize the importance of the preparation period as anyone who passes through this period cannot fail in their ministry.

When Apostle Paul came from Arabia, he was very much equipped, and his ministry could never be underestimated.

Greater reputation.

The church is an institution that is called to shine as the light to the whole world. The Bible compared it to a city build on a hill. Everyone can see it even from far, "*You are the light of the world. A city that is set on a hill cannot be hidden.* Let your light Shine!

> **"Nor do they light a lamp and put it under a basket, but on a lampstand, and it gives light to all who are in the house. Let your light so shine before men that they may see your good works and glorify your Father in heaven." (Mathew 5:14-16)**

If the church's image is tarnished because of poor leadership, it affects the entire mission of the church of evangelism and winning of souls.

Finally, any church needs to invest in teaching its leaders as this is key in fulfilling the Great Commission of Jesus Christ.

5 POINTS I HAVE LEARNED IN MY JOURNEY TO GOING GLOBAL

1 ______________________________

2 ______________________________

3 ______________________________

4 ______________________________

5 ______________________________

CHAPTER 23

Equip, Train, And Release Other Leaders

BE IT PROFESSIONAL OR religious; any institution should have well-planned strategies for equipping, training and releasing leaders. This is majorly for the benefit of the continuity of the visions and goals in that particular institution.

This is also applicable in a church set up. A well-structured religious denomination should put in place mechanisms of equipping, training, and releasing leaders. If that is not the case, there are less chances of continuity.

The church being the body of Christ, has been in existence for more than 2000 years ago since Jesus Christ ascended into heaven.

During the 3 years of the ministry of Jesus Christ, He made sure that training, equipping, and releasing His disciples is effectively done.

We will look at every aspect of the three and their importance in any growing institution.

Equipping

The word equip means to furnish for service against a need or prepare someone with a specific skill. From the definition, it clearly shows that equipping arises because of the necessity of a need.

There is a great need in many areas of service in the Church's' context to win souls.

> **"Then He said to them, the harvest truly is great, but the laborers are few; therefore pray the Lord of the harvest to send out laborers into His harvest." (Luke 10:2).**

Before the souls are won, there is a whole process of coordination of all departments involved in winning the souls. There is the part of the administration, the support team, and the delivery of the gospel.

This is the main reason why God, in His wisdom, makes sure that the body of Christ is equipped with all gifts that the church needs for effective ministry.

> "And He Himself gave some to be apostles, some prophets, some evangelists, and some pastors and teachers, ***for the equipping of the saints for the work of ministry***, for the edifying of the body of Christ," (Ephesians 4:11-12).

The benefits of equipping church and other leaders

A leader is someone that is looked up to, and a lot is expected from them. Equipping involves availing the necessary inputs that the lease will need to carry out their duties effectively. This is why in the above verse Jesus Christ has made sure that the church tasked in winning souls' mission has at hand the ministries of apostleship, prophets, evangelists, pastors, and teachers. The following are the reason for the equipping of leaders.

- **For the Body of Christ's edification:** The church is the body of Christ with varied needs. Without it being equipped, it won't function fully. This applies to any part of leadership, whether big or small. There must be a section that is responsible for equipping for service. For an army to be fully functional, it needs to have all the necessary weapons at its disposal. They should be availed before the army sets its foot to war; otherwise, it can never win any war. The church is compared to a soldier's life; there is a battle of winning souls that we need to find equipped soldiers to win.
- **For the Ministry's stability:** Well-equipped ministers are stable and cannot be shaken with any form of attack.

"Till we all come to the unity of the faith and of the knowledge of the Son of God, to a perfect man, to the measure of the stature of the fullness of Christ; ***that we should no longer be children, tossed to and fro and carried about with every wind of doctrine, by the trickery of men, in the cunning craftiness of deceitful plotting,*** " (Ephesians 4:13-14)

- **For growth:** Equipping the church leaders is creating room for growth. Every church would desire its members to grow and develop rather than being stagnant. Growth shows the effectiveness of any ministry; it also brings hope for the future and continuity. *But, speaking the truth in love,* ***may grow up in all things into Him who is the head—Christ—***

"From whom the whole body, joined and knit together by what every joint supplies, according to the effective working by which every part does its share causes growth of the body for the edifying of itself in love." (Ephesians 4:15-16).

Training

Training is the activity of imparting and acquiring skills. Good leaders are those that lead with skills. Any skilled leadership becomes effective and becomes easier to achieve intended results.

When Jesus Christ was electing His disciples, He assured them something; He was ready to make them.

"Then Jesus said to them, "Follow Me, ***and I will make you*** become fishers of men. They immediately left their nets and followed Him." (Mark 1:17-18).

Making is a process; it involves training to perfection. Jesus Christ knew that for His disciples to carry out His ministry, they must undergo thorough training. At times, during His ministry, He could have gotten annoyed - whenever He could see them not able to do some of the ministry work or lacked faith. He knew that it was His duty to make sure that they are thoroughly trained.

The writer of the book of Hebrews also could have gotten annoyed - when he couldn't see any growth in the believers he ministered to as he knew that he was responsible for training them.

"For though by this time you ought to be teachers, you need someone to teach you again the first principles of the oracles of God; and you have come to need milk and not solid food." (Hebrew 5:12)

The benefit of training church and other leaders

Training leaders have a lot of benefit to their areas of service. These are some of the benefits of training leaders.

- **For effectiveness**- A trained leader is more effective compared to an untrained one. Our God is a God of perfection and needs things to be done with perfection. David the psalmist considered this fact when he wrote; *"Sing Him a* *new song;* ***Play skillfully*** *with a shout of joy."* (Psalms 33:3) Apostle Paul instructs Timothy to study the word of God for effectiveness; Study and be eager and do your utmost to present yourself to God approved (tested by trial), **a workman who has no cause to be ashamed, correctly analyzing and accurately dividing [rightly handling and skillfully teaching] the Word of Truth**. (2 Timothy 2:15 AMP)

- **For empowerment**- Training leaders is a way of empowering them as they say that knowledge is power. Empowered leadership is a strong leadership that cannot be easily shaken.

Releasing out leaders

After equipping and training leaders, the last step is to send them out or release them for ministry. If this last step is missing in any institution, the whole process will not be complete.

As our perfect example of a good leader, Jesus Christ, after equipping and training His disciples, it was the time to send them out. Sending the trained leaders is a way of testing or examining to which level they have acquired their knowledge and training.

> "And He called the twelve to Himself, and began to send them out two by two, and gave them power over unclean spirits. He commanded them to take nothing for the journey except a staff—no bag, no bread, no copper in their money belts—but to wear sandals and not to put on two tunics. "Also, He said to them, "In whatever place you enter a house, stay there till you depart from that place. And whoever will not receive you nor hear you, when you depart from there, shake off the dust under your feet as a testimony against

them. Assuredly, I say to you; it will be more tolerable for Sodom and Gomorrah in the day of judgment than for that city! "So they went out and preached that people should repent." (Mark 6:7-12)

The benefit of sending out leaders

These are some of the benefits of sending out leaders after a period of equipping and training.

- **For sharpening the acquired skills:** Most of what is acquired during the training and equipping period needs to be put into practice. When leaders are sent out, it helps them sharpen their skills. When Jesus Christ sent the twelve out and returned with a good report, He knew very well that they were becoming ready to face mission work.
- **For multiplication and growth:** Leaders who are not sent out cannot grow in their areas of service. They need to step out to venture into new fields to learn the challenges that are outside there; this will, in turn, bring tremendous growth to the leaders.
- **Develops confidence in the leaders**- When a leader steps out for service for the first time, they might experience some fear of service or nervousness, which is normal. Still, the moment they send out regularly, it will create confidence in them. This confidence is most important as it raises someone's self-esteem and courage. This will, in turn, affect their ministry positively.

5 POINTS I HAVE LEARNED IN MY JOURNEY TO GOING GLOBAL

1 ______________________________

____

2 ______________________________

____

3 ______________________________

____

4 ______________________________

____

5 ______________________________

____

PART TWO

CHAPTER 24

Live A Life Of Cause

LIFE SHOULD NOT BE lived aimlessly but with a purpose. This is through the understanding that every individual exists with a purpose. No one exists by accident or chance; before the foundations of the earth were laid, God gave every individual a purpose to fulfill in life.

It is unfortunate that people have been born, lived, and eventually died without realizing their purpose in life. That is why one preacher said that the richest place on earth is the cemetery. As in the cemetery lies dreams that were never discovered and fulfilled. This is why Moses had to cry to the Lord in this prayer;

> **"So teach us to number our days, That we may gain a heart of wisdom." (Psalms 90:12).**

We should all be asking God to teach us to number our days, not to determine our years but for the sake of gaining a heart of wisdom. This means that if we knew that we have a few days to live here on earth, we will live a careful life and not waste any day.

If God could reveal to us the number of remaining days before we die, we could carefully live on this earth. We could maximize every second, minute, hour, and day in our lives.

This is what happened to Hezekiah.

> **"In those days, Hezekiah was sick and near death. And Isaiah the prophet, the son of Amoz, went to him and said to him, "Thus says the Lord: 'Set your house in order, for you shall die and not live.'" Then Hezekiah turned his face toward the wall, and prayed to the Lord, and said, "Remember now, O Lord, I pray, how I have walked before You in truth and with a loyal heart, and have done what is good in Your sight." And Hezekiah wept bitterly. And the word of the Lord came to Isaiah, saying, "Go and tell Hezekiah, 'Thus says the Lord, the God of David your father: "I have heard your prayer, I have seen your tears; surely I will add to your days fifteen years." (Isaiah 38:5).**

Jesus Christ only had a chance to live 33 years on this earth, but the impact He left on this earth is felt to date. This is because he was more focused on the will and purpose that His Father had sent Him to do. Let's see some of the statements Jesus Christ made to show that He was much focused and determined to accomplish His purpose on this earth.

> "Jesus said to them, "My food is to ***do the will of Him who sent Me and to finish His work.***" (John 4:34)

> But He said to them, "Let us go into the next towns, that I may preach there also ***because for this purpose I have come forth.***" (Mark 1:38)

> "Now My soul is troubled, and what shall I say? 'Father, save Me from this hour'? ***But for this purpose, I came to this hour.***" (John 12:27).

How to fulfill your purpose in life

Walk in wisdom

> "Therefore do not be unwise, but understand what the will of the Lord is." (Ephesians 5:17)

It takes wisdom for one to understand their purpose and the will of the Lord in their lives.

The good thing is that God is so faithful and very willing to give wisdom to anyone that asks God for it.

> "If any of you lacks wisdom, let him ask of God, who gives to all liberally and without reproach, and it will be given to him." (James 1:5)

David, the psalmist, understood this fact very well, which is to be prayed like this.

Show me Your ways, O Lord;
Teach me Your paths.
Lead me in Your truth and teach me,
For You are the God of my salvation;
On You, I wait all the day. (Psalms 25:4-5).

Not conforming to the patterns of this world.

This world is so deceptive and easily draws many from achieving their purpose in life. That is why believers are encouraged not to love the world and the things of the world.

> "Do not love the world or the things in the world. If anyone loves the world, the love of the Father is not in him. For all that is in the world—***the lust of the flesh, the lust of the eyes, and the pride of life***—is not of the Father but is of the world. And the world is passing away, and the lust of it; ***but he who does the will of God abides forever.***" (1 John 2:15-17).

From the above scriptures, we see that the world uses three powerful weapons to deceive man and try to make him not to achieve his purpose in life. After the baptism of Jesus Christ, He was led immediately to the wilderness by the Spirit to be tempted. The devil tempted Him in these three areas that we have mentioned.

- **The lust of the flesh**: (Matthew 4:2) *"And when He had fasted forty days, and forty nights, afterward He was hungry. Now when the tempter came to Him, he said, "If You are the Son of God, command that these stones become bread."* (Mathew 4:2-3). The devil knew very well that Jesus Christ had fasted for forty days and was very hungry. His flesh was at the test; will it allow to give in sin and miss the purpose of God? But the good news is that Jesus Christ was much focused on His purpose. He says in the book of John; Jesus said to them, *"My food is to do the will of Him who sent Me and to finish His work."* (John 4:34).

- **The lust of the eye**: *"Again, the devil took Him up on an exceedingly high mountain and* ***showed Him*** *all the kingdoms of the world and their glory. And he said to Him, "All these things I will give You if You will fall down and worship me."* (Mathew 4:8-9). We should be very careful at what the devil brings to our eyes. His tricks are to make us fall. Jesus Christ also overcame this temptation.
- **The pride of life**: (*Matthew 4:5) "Then the devil took Him up into the holy city, set Him on the pinnacle of the temple, and said to Him, "If You are the Son of God, throw Yourself down. For it is written: 'He shall give His angels charge over you, 'and, 'In their hands, they shall bear you up, Lest you dash your foot against a stone.'"*(Mathew 4:5-6). Jesus Christ also overcame this temptation.

Apostle Paul warns the church in Rome that if they want to prove God's perfect will, they should not be conformed to this world's patterns. *"And do not be conformed to this world, but be transformed by the renewing of your mind, that you may prove what is that good and acceptable and perfect will of God."* (Romans 12:2)

Abiding in the true Vine

Jesus Christ is the true Vine; in other words, He is the reason why we can achieve all our purpose in life. Minus Jesus Christ, you cannot achieve anything in life.

> "I am the vine; you are the branches. He who abides in Me, and I in him, bears much fruit; ***for without Me, you can do nothing.*** (John 15:5).

Jesus Christ himself distributed spiritual gifts to us to enable us to use the gift to achieve our purpose here on Earth. *Therefore He says:*

> "When He ascended on high, He led captivity captive, And gave gifts to men." (Ephesians 4:8).

Redeeming our time

Redeeming time is making maximum use of the time that one has been given to live in this world. Apostle Peter confesses that indeed they had spent enough time doing what they were not called to do. So after believing it was time to redeem the time that was lost in doing the will of the Gentiles.

> "For we have spent enough of our past lifetime in doing the will of the Gentiles—when we walked in lewdness, lusts, drunkenness, revelries, drinking parties, and abominable idolatries." (1 Peter 4:3).

Believers in Christ Jesus should realize that they are now in the light and should now walk as people of the light.

"For you were once darkness, but now you are light in the Lord. Walk as children of light." (Ephesians 5:8)

Jesus answered, *"Are there not twelve hours in the day? If anyone walks in the day, he does not stumble because he sees the light of this world. But if one walks in the night, he stumbles because the light is not in him."*(John 11:9-10)

If believers in Christ Jesus apply these principles on how to live a life of purpose, they will be effective in their area of calling and will definitely fulfill their God-given purpose in life. Because during the day of judgment, everyone will give an account of the days that he ever lived here on earth.

"So then each of us shall give account of himself to God." (Romans 24:12)

5 POINTS I HAVE LEARNED IN MY JOURNEY TO GOING GLOBAL

1 ______________________________

____

2 ______________________________

____

3 ______________________________

____

4 ______________________________

____

5 ______________________________

____

CHAPTER 25

Sharpen Your Message, Develop Your Ministry, Secure Your Mantle

"...See that you fulfill the ministry that you have received in the Lord." (Colossians 4:17...)

EVERY LEADER HAS A message. Your message must be unique, simplified, and clear. It is your message that makes you stand out. There is no single man that is sent all the messages of this life. Every messenger is sent with a unique message, and this is relative to an individual's audience, gifts, and scope.

Clarity is vital in your message. People shouldn't be confused about who you are and what you stand for. If you are clear about your message, it won't be difficult for people to figure out your uniqueness. In the bid to become impressive to people, leaders often lose their message. Your uniqueness gives you the worthiness of attention. It is not enough to have a message; you should have a uniqueness that can give you an edge in your niche. After this, you need to be compelling in your message. When your message is compelling, it increases your impact on your audience.

We do not need to be in full-time ministry to serve God. Not all of us would serve God in full-time ministry. Still, most of us would advance God's Kingdom through our professions, church engagements, community services, volunteering, families, and skills. The general perspective of an average believer is that only those in full-time ministries are serving God. This is a gross misconception. Ministry means service, and we are to serve God in whatever capacity, be it our homes, professions, occupation, or skill. The Bible says,

> **"For we are his workmanship, created in Christ Jesus for good works, which God prepared beforehand, that we should walk in them." (Ephesians 2:10 ESV).**

Since we are created for good works, we must allow people to see our light and give glory to God. The ultimate purpose of our ministry is to bring glory to God. The Bible says,

> "Let your light so shine before men that they may see your moral excellence and your praiseworthy, noble, and good deeds and recognize and honor and praise and glorify your Father Who is heaven." (Matthew 5:16 AMP).

To develop your ministry, there is a demand that you allow God to do it. The Bible says,

> "...on this rock, I will build my church..." (Matthew 16:18).

He is the sole builder of the church. The church is the body of Christ, and you are a member of that body. The church is also the system of operation of God's Kingdom on earth. Your ministry is a subset of God's operation on the earth. The Bible says,

> "For every house is built by someone, but God is the builder of everything." (Hebrew 3:4 NIV).

You must submit to God to build you. God needs you to build. He needs you as an instrument to build the ministry He has committed into your hands. Your goal should be to do God's pleasure. Your willingness to obey God's instructions and do things in God's way is important to the development of your ministry.

Furthermore, you must be ready to get off the scene for God to be seen. Jesus was the Father's express image, but He maintained a posture that brings us to see the Father, not Him. You should decide to allow God to be seen and glorified in all, and you would have Him lift you.

Also, it is important to teach with uniqueness, clarity, and relevance. Your ministry must be relevant to your audience, to the current season, and to civilization. The Bible says,

> **"For David, after he had served his generation by the will of God, fell on sleep, and was laid unto his fathers, and saw corruption." (Acts 13:36 KJV).**

David served God and served his generation, and not another's. Every generation has its uniqueness, and as a leader, you must know that you cannot serve a generation you are not sent to. Your ministry should communicate the message God gave you with relevance within the context of your society and needs. When it comes to content, relevance is very important. Intent alone is not enough in ministry; the content must be well packaged with value and excellence.

In developing ministry, you also need to develop others. You must be willing and available to invest in others. The work of the ministry needs the service of different people for perfection. The Bible says,

> **"So Christ himself gave the apostles, the prophets, the evangelists, the pastors, and teachers, to equip his people for works of service, so that the body of Christ may be built up until we all reach unity in faith and in the knowledge of the Son of God and become mature, attaining to the whole measure of the fullness of Christ." (Ephesians 4:11-13 NIV).**

You can develop your ministry by giving platforms for others to serve and pouring into others' lives. Then you must be able to develop them to become representatives of your ministry. Jesus trained the disciples and sent them to represent Him. They eventually became the pioneers and witnesses of His ministry. As you do this, you secure your mantle and place in God and the ministry He has called you into.

5 POINTS I HAVE LEARNED IN MY JOURNEY TO GOING GLOBAL

1 ____

____

2 ____

____

3 ____

____

4 ____

____

5 ____

____

CHAPTER 26

Be Yourself

IN SOME INSTANCES, IT is practically impossible for any business entrepreneur to survive without joining positive and Godly influenced associations. Because it has a way of networking and recognizing some prominent people in the business world, you get to meet some important personalities, relate with them, learn from them, and even be exposed to some rare opportunities.

For a Christian business entrepreneur who wants to be known globally, you might need to join such associations. Still, then you begin to wonder if belonging to these clubs is sinful because they are mostly filled with unbelievers, those who do not believe in the same faith as you. Sometimes in these associations and clubs, you might even be the only Christian, and you are surrounded by unbelievers who do not care about what you believe in. Then you begin to see the disadvantages and negativity in joining; doubts begin to crowd your mind about such organizations. The Bible in 2 Corinthians 6: 14 says

> **"Be ye not unequally yoked together with unbelievers; for what fellowship has righteousness with unrighteousness? And what communion hath light with darkness?"**

When a verse like this comes to your mind, you feel like there is no need to associate yourself with unbelievers or even partner with them in business. To be yoked together means adopting their lifestyle, ideology, and belief system. Is there really a way of belonging to these business clubs and fraternities without being unequally yoked with unbelievers? Of course, there is! You can just avoid worldly associations and be yourself. Note, however, that there may be times when you may be invited to attend certain business functions and socials with persons from all walks of life – that will allow your business to grow or improve. This depends on your business area, e.g., if you work in the tourism arena or service. Again just be yourself.

What does it mean to be you?

Being yourself is one factor that allows you to associate with unbelievers without being influenced by their lifestyle but instead allowing your life to change them preferably.

Being yourself has to do with not allowing anything to influence your character and your way of life. Before any man can *"be himself,"* he/she must have a standard or a way of life that he is abiding by; you must have some specific principles you set for your life (something you are living for and the things you cannot engage yourself in). Any man that has not defined his purpose cannot *"be himself,"* and he/she would allow the different circumstances around him to pressure himself to what he is not.

For example, as a Christian entrepreneur, you have to make up your mind on some things you can engage yourself in and things you cannot engage yourself with. This is because they are against your faith and your lifestyle. When there is a clear definition of 'who you are' and 'what you do,' you can now maintain being yourself without allowing compromise.

Being around an unbeliever (in such context) is no sin; in fact, it was recorded that Jesus received and ate with sinners (Luke 15: 2). The fact that Jesus ate with them makes us understand that Jesus was not running away from sinners; he wanted to make them understand that he had to come to save them. He knew who he was, and so He defined how His relationship with unbelievers would be so He could save them. In such an instance, you can be a light.

Knowing 'who you are' and being 'what you are' would make you see that those associations do not mean you are sinning. But there is a need for caution. You will begin to see that there are things that you have to change. As such, management of the clubs or the people's lives also needs to be changed.

Wherever we are in life, we would always be surrounded by unbelievers whom we cannot run away from; and so if it comes to the fact that we would need to partner with them to a certain extent, we must do so. Not to allow them to influence your lifestyle and standards but for you to be who you are and use your life to influence them to Christ. Know who you are in Christ and be yourself!

Build and expand your networks by joining organizations or groups with Christian values – and values of your own. You can meet with global individuals to partner in business. Partnership is very important to big successful companies, and if you want to rise to a global level. In some cases, such association may be beneficial.

5 POINTS I HAVE LEARNED IN MY JOURNEY TO GOING GLOBAL

1 ____________________

2 ____________________

3 ____________________

4 ____________________

5 ____________________

CHAPTER 27

Loving People

What is love?

Love is a strong affection towards something or someone. It is the greatest commandment in the Bible and also a fruit of the Holy Spirit.

What is the origin of love?

Before the universe ever existed, there was love. This is because God existed before creation, and God himself is love. *He who does not love does not know God, for God is love.* (1 John 4:8)

Why do we love?

1. *It is the first and the greatest commandment.*

> **"Teacher, which is the great commandment in the law?" Jesus said to him, "You shall love the Lord your God with all your heart, with all your soul, and with all your mind." This is the first and great commandment. (Mathew 22:36-37)**

2. *It is a way to inherit eternal life.*

When a certain lawyer met Jesus Christ and asked Him what to do to inherit eternal life, Jesus had to answer him like this; *So he answered and said, "'You shall love the Lord your God with all your heart, with all your soul, with all your strength, and with all your mind,' and 'your neighbor as yourself.'"* (Luke 10:27).

3. It is an evidence of our knowledge of God

Because God is love, when we love people, it is a way to show that we know God.

> **Beloved, let us love one another, for love is of God; *and everyone who loves is born of God and knows God.* He who does not love does not know God, for God is love. (1 John 4:7-8).**

We have the love of man that is directed towards God and the love of man towards man. The two go hand in hand. You cannot claim to love God if you can't love your brother.

> "If someone says, "I love God," and hates his brother, he is a liar; for he who does not love his brother whom he has seen, how can he love God whom he has not seen? And this commandment we have from Him: ***that he who loves God must love his brother also.***" (1 John 4:20-21).

In this article, we will focus on the love of humans towards their fellow humans.

Characteristics of True love.

The word Love is one of the most abused words in the world. Some people use it when they are referring to the word lust. This has sometimes caused suffering to people to whom the word love has been wrongly used. Love should be accompanied by its deeds.

> "My little children, let us not love in word or in tongue, but indeed and in truth." (John 3:18)

These are some of the characteristics of true love.

> "Love ***suffers long*** and is ***kind***; love ***does not envy;*** love ***does not parade itself***, is ***not puffed up***; ***does not behave rudely, does not seek its own,*** is ***not provoked, thinks no evil; does not rejoice in iniquity,*** but rejoices in the truth; ***bears all things, believes all things, hopes all things, endures all things. Love never fails.*** But whether there are prophecies, they will fail; whether there are tongues, they will cease; whether there is knowledge, it will vanish away." (1 Corinthians 13:4-8).

We will be looking at each characteristic of love with the intention of learning from it.

Love suffers long.

The meaning of the word long-suffering is never getting tired of waiting (patient). If you really love someone, you must be read to wait no matter how long it would take. This is what Jesus Christ is doing to the lost mankind. He loves the whole world to the extent that He is not coming quickly before they believe in Him and get saved. He is waiting for all to be saved as He can't afford to lose even one soul because of love.

> **"*The Lord* is not slack concerning His promise, as some count slackness, but is *longsuffering* toward us, not willing that any should perish but that all should come to repentance." (2 Peter 3:9)**

Love is kind.

Kindness is the act of displaying charitable behavior towards people around you. The Bible calls it brotherly kindness. Apostle Peter encourages believers to possess brotherly kindness, "*To godliness brotherly kindness, and to brotherly kindness love.*" (2 Peter 1:7). This clearly shows that you cannot claim to love without showing kindness to people.

Love doesn't envy.

Envy and love cannot go hand in hand. Those who claim to love cannot, at the same time, be envious. The Bible says in the book of Proverbs that "*A sound heart is a life to the body,*

But envy is rottenness to the bones." (Proverbs 14:30).

Love does not parade itself.

True love does not display itself. Acts of kindness or charity accompany most acts of love. Jesus Christ taught His disciples that as we carry out acts of kindness, we should never show off

> **"Take heed that you do not do your charitable deeds before men, to be seen by them. Otherwise, you have no reward from your Father in heaven. Therefore, when you do a charitable deed, do not sound a trumpet before you as the hypocrites do in the synagogues and in the streets, that they may have glory from men. Assuredly, I say to you; they have their reward. "But when you do a charitable deed, do not let your left hand know what your right hand is doing, that your charitable deed may be in secret; and your Father who sees in secret will Himself reward you openly." (Matthew 6: 1-4).**

Love is not puffed up.

Puffing up is boasting. Puffing is a result of pride, wanting to show that you are better than others. *But He gives more grace. Therefore He says:*

> **"God resists the proud, But gives grace to the humble." (James 4:6).**

God is never pleased with pride as it is never motivated by love.

Apostle Paul gives a perfect example of humility from the life of Jesus Christ. He shows how Jesus Christ left glory and splendor in heaven and because of us. The humility in Jesus Christ made Him lower Himself to the point of accepting to be born in the appearance of man and dying a painful death at the cross.

"Let this mind be in you which was also in Christ Jesus, who, being in the form of God, did not consider it robbery to be equal with God, but made Himself of no reputation, taking the form of a bondservant, and coming in the likeness of men. And being found in appearance as a man, ***He humbled Himself and became obedient to the point of death, even the death of the cross.***" (Philippians 2:5-8)

Love does not behave rudely.

You can't be rude and, at the same time, show love. Love humbles someone and makes him gentle. Look at the example of Jesus Christ. Although He was God, He never disrespected the governing authorities during His time. Christ doesn't resist his arrest and trial, neither His crucifixion. He does this because of the love He had for the lost world.

For this, you were called because Christ also suffered for us, leaving us an example that you should follow His steps: "Who committed no sin, Nor was deceit found in His mouth; ***who, when He was reviled, did not revile in return; when He suffered, He did not threaten, but committed Himself to Him who judges righteously;***"(1 Peter 2:21-23).

Perfect love is unconditional; it doesn't depend on the recipient but gentle.

"Repay no one evil for evil. Have regard for good things in the sight of all men. If it is possible, as much as depends on you, live peaceably with all men." (Romans 12: 17-18)

Love doesn't think of evil nor rejoices in iniquity.

An evil mind can never produce love, as love and evil can never exist together. An evil mind is only a breeding place of every sort of iniquity, which leads to sin. As the Bible says that whoever sins is of the devil and not of God as God is love.

> **"But each one is tempted when he is drawn away by his own desires and enticed. Then, when desire has conceived, it gives birth to sin; and sin, when it is full-grown, brings forth death." (James 1:14-15).**

> **"But he who hates his brother is in darkness, walks in darkness, and does not know where he is going because the darkness has blinded his eyes." (1 John 2:11).**

If we abide by the above biblical principles, we will not find it hard to love the people around us.

> **"To godliness, brotherly kindness, and to brotherly kindness love. For if these things are yours and abound, you will be neither barren nor unfruitful in the knowledge of our Lord Jesus Christ." (2 Peter 1:7-8).**

> **And now abide faith, hope, love, these three; but the greatest of these is love. (1 Corinthians 13:13)**

5 POINTS I HAVE LEARNED IN MY JOURNEY TO GOING GLOBAL

1 ______________________________

____

2 ______________________________

____

3 ______________________________

____

4 ______________________________

____

5 ______________________________

____

CHAPTER 28

Empower Your Followers

WHEN YOU ARE A leader, much is expected of you; this part is obvious that people expect you to provide better leadership. But also, there is the part of empowering and equipping the people you lead.

They say that a good leader natures and leaves behind leaders. This means that anyone in a leadership position will make sure that the people they lead can do exactly or more than what he does. This is what we call empowerment. It is one of the greatest principles of leadership.

What empowerment entails

Delegation of duties.

For someone to do a particular thing, he/ she must have been given a chance to do it at some time. Some leaders fear delegating duties because of the fear of competition. But that should not be the case; any leader should be free to delegate his duties to their subjects. This is a form of training and equipping leaders.

While carrying out His earthly ministry, Jesus Christ knew very well that He will not always be present with His disciples physically. He knew that time would come when He will be going back to His father. To make sure that He leaves behind leaders that would continue with His ministry, He chose the seventy and sent them out.

> **"After these things, the Lord appointed seventy others also and sent them two by two before His face into every city and place *where He Himself was about to go.*" (Luke 10:1)**

The Bible records that Jesus Christ sent the seventy to every place and city that He was about to go. Meaning that they were to perform exactly what His Father had sent Him to do. Jesus Christ didn't give them a lesser task. This means that He was empowering them and making them ready for the future mission.

And the result was evident; this was the report that the seventy came with.

> **"Then the seventy returned with joy, saying, "Lord, even the demons are subject to us in Your name." And He said to them, "I saw Satan fall like lightning from heaven. Behold, I give you the authority to**

trample on serpents and scorpions, and over all the power of the enemy, and nothing shall by any means hurt you." (Luke 10:17-19).

Serving as an example

Your subjects or the people that you lead will always follow what the leader does. This is because some will learn through imitation. This, therefore, calls for all leaders to serve as a good example to everyone. Bad leadership can be handed over easily as some characters can be easily passed down from leaders to their subjects.

When Jesus Christ wanted to teach His disciples about serving one another, He had to demonstrate it by being the example.

"Jesus, knowing that the Father had given all things into His hands, and that He had come from God and was going to God, rose from supper and laid aside His garments, took a towel and girded Himself. After that, He poured water into a basin and began to wash the disciples' feet and to wipe them with the towel with which He was girded." (John 133-5)

"So when He had washed their feet, taken His garments, and sat down again, He said to them, "Do you know what I have done to you?"" (John 13:12)

"You call Me Teacher and Lord, and you say well, for so I am. If I then, your Lord and Teacher, have washed your feet, you also ought to wash one another's feet. *For I have given you an example that you should do as I have done to you."* (John 13:13-15).

Jesus Christ also had to undergo suffering to leave an example to his followers, who would later face exactly what He went through. *"For to this, you were called, because Christ also suffered for us, leaving us an example, that you should follow His steps."* (1 Peter 2:21)

Being patient and giving your subjects time.

Leaders should learn that growth needs to be given time. Therefore they ought to be patient in every way if they want to achieve better results. This calls them to be exercise a lot of patience. Apostle Paul instills this principle in his son Timothy when he instructs him like this; *"And a servant of the Lord must not quarrel but be gentle to all, able to teach,* ***patient****,"* (2 Timothy 2:24).

Providing necessary resources.

For you to empower your followers, you must spend your resources on equipping them. When Apostle Paul was mentoring his son Timothy, he made sure that Timothy gets the right doctrine as he was expecting Timothy to rise up for ministry.

> **"If you instruct the brethren in these things, you will be a good minister of Jesus Christ, nourished in the words of faith *and of the good doctrine which you have carefully followed.*" (1 Timothy 4:6-7).**

Giving positive feedback

When Apostle Paul was in prison, he encountered a young man known as Onesimus, a runaway slave to Philemon. He mentors and transforms him from being unprofitable to profitable. When Paul releases him to go back to his master, he gives good feedback or reports about the transformation that Onesimus had undergone. We believe that when Onesimus heard how Apostle Paul praised him, he couldn't wait to be out of prison and continue with the ministry that Paul had taught him.

> "I appeal to you for my son Onesimus, whom I have begotten while in my chains, who once was unprofitable to you, but now is profitable to you and to me. I am sending him back. You therefore receive him, that is, my own heart, whom I wished to keep with me, that on your behalf he might minister to me in my chains for the gospel. But without your consent, I wanted to do nothing, that your good deed might not be by compulsion, as it were, but voluntary. For perhaps he departed for a while for this purpose, that you might receive him forever, ***no longer as a slave but more than a slave—a beloved brother, especially to me but how much more to you, both in the flesh and in the Lord.*** " (Philemon 1:10-16)

Recognition for the work done.

As you train and empower leaders, you need to recognize and commend those who have done exemplary work. This makes someone develop the urge to move on. Instead of always complaining when things go wrong, it is also good to recognize those that have performed well in the leadership training process.

Apostle Paul could not make it alone in his ministry; he had some people that he was training that stood beside him who played a big role in his ministry.

For him to empower them, he takes a whole chapter sixteen in the letter to the Romans to commend everyone who stood by him. A good leader should be talking about the wrong that his subjects do and praise them when they do good.

Practicing forgiveness.

One of the greatest virtue that should be practiced in empowering your followers is the act of forgiving. When the people that you are mentoring make mistakes, they should be forgiven. This is because forgiveness is passed over.

When Jesus Christ was teaching His disciples how to pray, He said; *"And forgive us our debts, As we forgive our debtors."* (Mathew 6:12). The parable of the unforgiving servant clearly shows the effects of not forgiving. (Mathew 18:21-35).

Benefits of empowering your followers

It allows individual growth.

Empowered individuals can easily grow and develop their ability as empowerment motivates individuals to move on to greater heights. In turn, this will be a benefit to any leader.

It makes one accountable

Empowerment increases accountability because when one is delegated duties to perform on their own, they tend to be careful.

Increases confidence and creativity

When leaders empower their subjects, they increase confidence in them and make them more innovative.

Examples of leaders in the Bible that rose because of empowerment

Under Elijah's leadership, Elisha rose to become a great prophet and leader who did a lot because he was empowered.

- The twelve disciples of Jesus Christ did many exploits as recorded in the book of Acts because Jesus Christ had empowered them before Him going back to Heaven.

- Timothy rose and became a good teacher of God's word as a result of Apostle Paul empowering and walking with Him.

Therefore we can conclude that there is a great benefit when leaders empower the people they lead as the time will come when they will be required to leave their office. It would be better to mentor someone as leadership is passed on from one person to the other.

> **"And the things that you have heard from me among many witnesses, commit these to faithful men who will be able to teach others also." (2 Timothy 2:2)**

5 POINTS I HAVE LEARNED IN MY JOURNEY TO GOING GLOBAL

1 ____

2 ____

3 ____

4 ____

5 ____

CHAPTER 29

Relating To New People With Language And Culture Barriers

How does it feel walking in a new environment, and you can't express yourself well? This can be the most nerve-wracking situation in your life. Cultural differences restrain proper communication due to various languages and symbols. The way everyone communicates gets defined by the environment they grew in. When we grow up, we meet or work with people from diversified cultures.

Sometimes, we even get into romantic relationships with them. In such situations, it can lead to a sea of confusion if you cannot share your thoughts verbally. It is also challenging if you cannot express yourself in the restaurant for the correct order. Online interactions like Zoom connection or any other video conferencing are not viable without suitable communication. Here are valuable tips on how to improve communication across cultural and language barriers.

Understand Different Body Languages

In the world, various cultures use different nonverbal signs to converse. For instance, some African communities may prefer shaking hands with strangers. In another part of the planet, the Chinese people would appreciate a nod. In some other cases, people in western countries' smiles are illuminated through the eyes. In return, the easterners brighten their eyes when meeting other people and may opt not to smile. When completing these people for the first time, you need to do a background check to avoid offending any.

Respect Personal Space

Another significant variance among cultures is maintaining personal space. Different communities and religions vary on these. For example, Muslim men and women are not allowed to worship in the same area. In other cities, it is not fitting to touch one another. At the same time, countries in South America like Peru do not mind getting closer to strangers. In Arab countries and part of Turkey, it is almost a taboo to get that close. This can result in a dilemma when people from these regions meet. Coming into common grounds may not be easy. Either way, you can introduce a barrier between them to avoid touching. What matters is their communication and not how they perceive each other.

Be Patient with One Another

There are a few incidents where you can presume what people want to say. But, it requires staying with someone for long to be able to complete each other sentences. In places like a restaurants, you are expected to communicate your order. In different informal settings, opinions with a new friend or colleague may differ. This is more noticeable when one is more conversant with the shared language than the other. Making a thought reach home may get almost impossible for both of them. To counter this, patience is required in simplifying conversations. If need be, one can enroll in classes to enhance their linguistic capability.

Do not forget to include an Expression

Even if body language comes in handy in a new environment, it can get misunderstood. Various nonverbal signs can aid in figuring out the context. Nevertheless, the tone of your voice can also guide someone on what you want to communicate. Through an expression, they can discern when you are sad or happy. For instance, someone can describe a type of distress through a sob. Those who come to assist may not understand the issue well, but it can be a start. The incorporation of body language and expression cut the language barrier by almost half.

Select Your Vocabulary

Due to various backgrounds, some people may have a different understanding of some words. For instance, a native speaker would recognize the phrase 'get up' as coming out of the bed. While someone else may relate it with the 'stand up phrase.'

To cross the bridge, you need to use a more straightforward vocabulary with these people. If possible, abstain from words that have similar meanings or sound almost the same. Try also to explain the importance of some hard words.

Keep off From Idioms

An idiom is an expression that is not easily understood from ordinary meaning. For example, you can say, "hit the nail on the head'. This does not mean the actual act of thumping. Instead, it explains, "you are precisely right." For an English speaker, idioms can sneak into conversations without noticing. They should be avoided when talking to a person from a different culture. Some of them are confusing to people who share a language but live in other countries. For example, the English spoken in New Zealand has some variances with Canada, the USA, and Britain.

Minimize the Humor

Humor is a way to ease up a situation, but sometimes it can lead to confusion. There are various cultural differences in humor. For example, humor is not a positive attitude in Japan, like in the United States. In other societies, sarcasm is not appreciated or used in any conversation. If you move to an environment where irony is the day's order, it can get confusing. The solution is to keep off from humor phases if you deal with someone not conversant with them.

Avoid Shouting

Most people in the world tend to repeat words to those not fluent in a specific language. Sometimes when the recipient fails to understand, they loudly repeat it in a firm tone. This only makes the situation worse and most unlikely to lead to any effective communication. Understanding of anything is never amplified with increased volume. Instead, what's needed is patience and clarity. You are only required to pronounce words easier without shouting. If there is an accent challenge, be patient in pronouncing them well. Avoid paraphrasing as it can confuse them more if you pronounce an unfamiliar word.

Practice Kindness

Compassion improves the quality of life in all aspects. When incorporated into communication, it brings different people together. Occasionally, you may fail to remember another person's taboos and disappoint them. For instance, you may get carried away by a conversation and pat an Arab lady on the back. At other times, you may include sarcasm into a conversation and irritate someone. Worse is even trying to simplify your talking for others to understand. All these are challenges brought up by cultural diversification. To face them well, you need to embrace politeness and kindness. Always seek forgiveness in case you irritate one another. In return, you will enjoy more significant conversations as a reward.

Concentrate on Understanding

Sometimes words may not have a definite translation. Put yourself in a situation where you want a new fabric for your lounge. You have mustard yellow as your theme color, but it is hard to explain it to someone who is not fluent. You are only left with the option of checking something similar online and showing them. The dissimilarity of mustard yellow and other types of yellow is very significant to you. You do not want to try another color. A phone illustration is an incredible option on how you can use other means of communication. But in rare cases, you may not have something to refer to. In such situations, you can choose to let go and conclude on something close to it.

How to Cut Through the Cultural Barriers

Communication and culture will always remain interrelated as each defines the other. We may not be able to dissect all the cultural challenges that hinder communication. But we can start by mentioning ways of increasing cultural knowledge as part of the solution. Here are four amusing ways of doing it.

Make Friends with People from Different Backgrounds

If you were not exposed to other communities in your early days, it might get uncomfortable to do it later in life. If we want to cut loose from the cultural rut, you need to seek out people from different backgrounds. By socializing with them, you can have a clear picture of why they behave the way they do. You can also embrace a holistic approach to global issues to understand what happens elsewhere.

Join in Cultural Events

To understand a particular tradition, you need to witness their celebrations and customs in person. When you have multi-racial friends, they can update you on special events. From watching Maasai dancing in Kenya to an Orthodox wedding in Russia, these events can take you all around. The attendance will make you value communal love shared across the globe.

Travel with an Intention

If you book yourself in an exotic place, don't just lie down sunbathing or golfing. You need to venture out of the room and experience the richness of the vicinity. By sampling the local cuisine to socializing with native, you learn so much. Practice openness to suck up the uniqueness of the different cultures into your own.

Study a New Language

There is immense satisfaction when you connect with different people through their language. The native language is very sentimental to the people who communicate with it. It does not matter how incoherent you sound, but the people will appreciate your efforts. Learning a new language is not easy, but it can help you win a great battle against cultural barriers.

5 POINTS I HAVE LEARNED IN MY JOURNEY TO GOING GLOBAL

1 ____

____

2 ____

____

3 ____

____

4 ____

____

5 ____

____

CHAPTER 30

You Are An Economy, Business, Currency

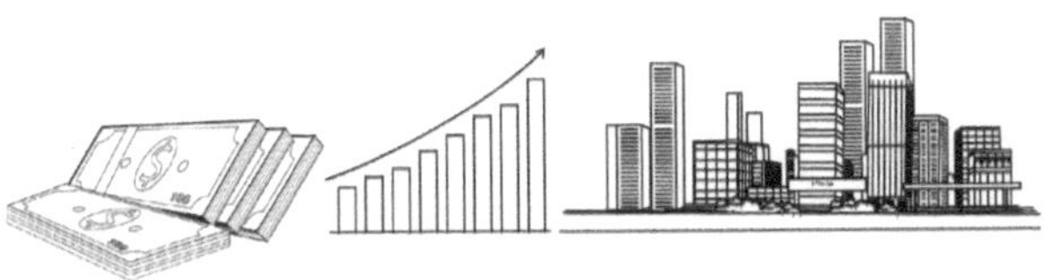

"Not slothful in business; fervent in spirit; serving the Lord." (Romans 12:11 KJV)

You are a person of great worth. You are in an economy; you are an economy. You are not in business; you are the business. You are not spending a currency; you are the currency. Your personality and uniqueness are your currency because no one else has your experience, gifts, skills, knowledge, perspective, and values. Focus o 'who' you are and what you have, rather than who others are and what they have that you do not have.

No one can do things you do the way you do them. You have valuable dreams, ideas, and beliefs. Your self-perception will lead to your self-projection, which will influence the way people see you and what they perceive about you. Opportunities come quite easily when people are attracted to your distinctiveness and uniqueness. A proper understanding of who you are will help you create something valuable. Your products are a function of the processes going on in your mind. When you are excellent minded, everything you do or produce will be birthed with excellence.

God-made Millionaire

The general conception of the public is that rich people are not Godly; it is the belief of the people of some parts of the world that riches must be acquired in deceit and trickery, and so it is hard for a Christian to be rich without taking these measures. But God gives wealth, and he gives it to his beloved people; there are millionaires that God has made today that are standing for the truth, and they did not get their wealth through fraudulent practices. Wealth and riches are our inheritance. The Bible says,

> **"You shall remember the Lord your God, for it is he who gives you power to get wealth, that he may confirm his covenant that he swore to your fathers, as it is this day." (Deuteronomy 8:18 ESV).**

No man can get wealth outside God. True wealth is a gift from God. God gives power, ideas, and blessings that can translate into wealth. After God created man, one of the commands he gave to him was to prosper and subdue the earth. The Bible says in Genesis 1:28

"...be fruitful, multiply and fill the earth, subdue it (using all its vast resources in the service of God and man)" (AMP)

"God blessed them; Prosper! Reproduce! Fill earth! Take charge..." (MSG)

The man God created is meant to take charge; man is meant to prosper. God created man with riches, and so a man can be prosperous in life and still be Godly. God wants Godly men in leadership; he wants men to take charge, be in control. Being a Christian does not make you mediocre. You can become a God - made millionaire by the blessings of God. It has been pronounced on you already. God has already pronounced his blessings upon you; you just have to know that you have been made rich by the blessings God has placed upon you.

God has a plan for every man to flourish and become prosperous; you can become a millionaire without involving yourself with the different atrocities that the people of the world involve themselves with. The Bible says,

"I will give you hidden treasures, riches stored in secret places, so that you may know that I am the Lord, the God of Israel, who summons you by name." (Isaiah 45:3 NIV).

This is your inheritance in God's Kingdom. There are treasures in hidden places; riches in secret places; and God, who cannot lie, has spoken that He has given them to you. You need to position yourself to receive the blessing by having certain attributes.

You cannot become a God made millionaire by accident; some attributes can make you harness God's riches

One of the ways one can become a God made millionaire is by diligence. The Bible says:

> **"Seest thou a man diligent in his business? He shall stand before Kings; and he shall not before mean men." (Proverbs 22:29).**

Hard work and diligence make a man receive God's blessings; he begins to experience exploits and accomplish different accomplishments under God. People begin to see his different accomplishments, and such a man does not stand before ordinary men or in ordinary places; such a man makes exploits globally. Diligence can change your audience, customers, and associates. Do you have a global dream? You cannot just sit around and wait for the dream to come true. You need to work, be diligent in deserving the blessing. Diligence takes your business from the local community to an international audience.

Even though God has blessed us, He desires that we are skilled in our business and work to reach the peak of our attainment. A Christian entrepreneur will take his brand or business globally if he is diligent and skilled in his works. When you have a particular job, you are exceptionally good at and have built your brand; you will activate the promise of God upon your life. Your riches would not be worldly (the one that lasts for a short while) but a God made prosperity that brings no sorrow or pain.

5 POINTS I HAVE LEARNED IN MY JOURNEY TO GOING GLOBAL

1 ______________________________

____

2 ______________________________

____

3 ______________________________

____

4 ______________________________

____

5 ______________________________

____

CHAPTER 31

Significance Of Online Platforms

ONLINE PLATFORMS ARE DIGITAL service that allows linking two or more co-dependent users through the Internet. They are crucial innovations in the digital world closely related to the success of businesses that use them. Buying goods, learning, networking, accessing content, and searching for information is now more accessible online. Individuals become dependent on them due to the improved efficiency, convenience, and competitiveness they have brought. Not only do they allow smaller companies to expand their operations, but they also increase civil involvement. 60% of the world is now digitalized, with around 4.56 billion users. Out of that figure, 3.8 billion are social media users. Below, we will discuss Facebook, Zoom, Video Conferencing, and Online teaching, and the role they play in the digital world.

Why use Facebook

Facebook is a popular social networking site that started running on 4th February 2004. It currently boasts close to 2.7 billion users from 2.38 billion in 2019, with a net worth of $744.22 billion. It presents an exceptional marketing opening for businesses through the innovation of business pages. Promotion on Facebook has a significant impact as information is stretched through networks all over the world. Marketing on Facebook is through the groups and the pages. Groups are focused on linking people who share similar interests. While in pages, users interact with a particular product or brand. Apart from providing a dialogue between a brand and consumers, it allows an organization to get quick feedback. Whenever a user becomes a fan of a page, a notice is posted for the friends to see. Through this, the page reaches new viewers. It is also used to create brand awareness for a modern audience, helping an organization reposition itself in fresh and distinctive ways. As the fan base grows, traffic to the connected company website increase as well. To create a business page, you need to have a personal profile. Each account can manage several business pages.

Creating a Personal Account

Click www.facebook.com/r.php. From there, type your name, mobile number, gender email, and date of birth. The next step is creating a password for security and helping you to sign up. To finish, you are required to confirm your phone number and email.

How to Create a Business Page

From your Facebook profile, go to http://www.facebook.com/pages/#/advertising/?pages for instructions. Press on "Create a Page" and fill in your brand details. Choose a category for your business from a public figure, band, artist, local, product, or brand. If you fill in your business as a product or brand, it is easier to add more information than a local business entry. Once the page is created, fill in the company information and upload a logo or image as your profile photo. From there, you need to include the edit and update section through the page manager. The section is at the bottom of the browser page. Click on the applications tab to view the current ones. To add more, click the view more tab to browse for extra applications. Note that not all apps are available for addition to the business page. Look for a notification from Facebook support saying, "You can add this application to some of your Facebook Pages." To promote your page, you need to build your fan base by reconnecting family, friends, clients, and associates by inviting them. Initiate a dialogue by posting persuasive content on the page to entice users. You can offer special promotions or inbox messages with promo codes for freebies or free invitations to events to encourage participation. It is crucial to maintain the page growth by repeat updates on events and news.

Why Use Zoom

Zoom is a cloud-based video app that was initiated on 21st April 2011 by Eric Yuan. Due to the Corona pandemic, Zoom has become the communication avenue for religious groups, federal governments, business startups, and regular persons. Around 200 million users in the world facilitate their meeting through the app in one day. This is a rise from 10million users and a net worth of $ 622.7 million last year. Zoom allows one to set up webinars, virtual video, auditory conferencing, screen sharing, live charts, and other capabilities. The great advantage of this platform is that you do not need to have an account to participate in a meeting. The app is effortlessly attuned with windows, Mac, Linux, Android, and iOS. It is light in weight with an interface connectable to standard features like Gallery View. This mode allows one to see each person on call.

How to Connect Through Zoom

Zoom offers four distinctive pricing arrangements from basic to enterprise. The categorization depends on your plans for the app. Zoom basic the most used tier, considering it comes free. It offers endless one-on-one meetings, but the video is limited to 40 minutes for three or more partakers. It is ideal for chatting with family and friends or for checking out the Zoom features. Zoom pro works for a small team and allows lengthened video calls to 24 hours. This plan enables the host to make IDs for other meetings and stores recorded content in the cloud. Zoom business accommodates at least ten people, perfect for small to medium companies. This tier comes with customer support, company branding, and an auto-generated transcript. The Zoom enterprise plan is designed for outsized organizations with a minimum of around 100 hosts. It includes various offers like boundless cloud storage, customer support manager, and competence of hosting 500 on one call.

Once you settle on a plan, download the app on your device. It is available for android, iPhone, and iPad devices through Google and App store. If working from your computer, download it from Zoom's official website. The process varies with the plan you choose. You may not require an account for a zoom meeting, but you have to sign up if you are hosting, managing, or scheduling calls. To join a meeting without an account, you can click the Zoom meeting link to get added in. Also, you can click on the homepage to enter manually. Alternatively, you can go through the Zoom supports dial-in calling if you do not have access to a desktop or the app. To program a meeting without an account, head to the app or the account page, click schedule, and proceed. You will be able to invite other participants via phone number, email, or contact. The easiest way to send a Zoom invite is by sharing the link you receive when you schedule a meeting.

Why Communicate Through Video Conferencing

Video conferencing was introduced in 1968 as a commercial solution in Network. It started as Picturephone AT&T, and currently, it is the closest substitute to face to face meetings with more than 12 million users daily worldwide. Grandview Research mentioned that the global market for video conferencing was about $ 3.85 billion in 2019. The estimated growth of 9.9% is expected by 2027. Video conferencing creates a forum that enables management to address issues and relay information quickly to employees. Effectual communication is critical to keep businesses running, especially during these difficult times. It plays a vital role in maintaining international employees and customers connected. Social distancing has encouraged organizations to transform their operations by including video connections. Video conferencing saves time and is more personalized. They provide users with convenience by allowing seamless connections with people in different time zones in the comfort of their homes. The majority of video platforms allow recordings, while others like Verbit offer live transcripts. Video conferencing allows fair participation to all staff and assists in the training of new employees.

How to Connect Through Video Conferencing

Simple, download the app, and choose your embedded webcam and microphone. Put on your headphones and connect to the virtual meeting room. Note that most meetings comprise at least a single meeting space for other groups to join. Web conferencing is recommended while solving the problem, as it does not have complicated conferencing networks. To set up a video link, you need a connected TV or display for presentation. Get a video conferencing system made up of a high definition camera and video processing codec. This receives and sends information and deciphers it live on the display. A conference phone which provides a user interface navigates the directory and launch calls. Conference phones and microphones allow automatic gain control and minimal noise for crystal clear audio. To connect for a meeting, you need to link the video system to the display. Pair the system with the life-size account and make your video conference call.

Importance of Online Teaching

Online education platforms started from the University of Illinois through an Intranet for its students in 1960. The Internet was not yet invented until nine years later. E-learning continues to spread out, offering a selection of knowledge tools to companies, individuals, and companies.

Before this, classes were limited to talks, physical materials, and lectures. Learners now have a choice between digital courses and textbooks. The combination of flexibility, low cost, and convenience transferred the global education value to an impressive $107 billion in 2015. It is estimated that the force will experience a tremendous increase value of $ 325 by 2025. Online materials now offer new bearing to modern society and professionalism. It allows easy access and sharing of information between students and teachers and a greater depth of understanding. It also provides an equal chance for people living with disabilities that restrict one-on-one lessons.

How to Teach Online

Teaching online allows a trainer to rethink and tackle classroom limitations. Knowledge is vital as an expert; you need to know more than the students. Get the facts right and analyze the importance of adapting them to an online class. There are various platforms to teach with, like Vedamo, Ruzuku, Teachable, Udemy, WizIQ, and many others. Vedamo is the most popular one and does not require downloading. It also allows a demo without creating an account. To improve online teaching, record the lessons, and do not stream them. Keep the videos short and utilize accessible resources. Make sure to give detailed instructions and offer interactive activities.

5 POINTS I HAVE LEARNED IN MY JOURNEY TO GOING GLOBAL

1 ______________________________

____

2 ______________________________

____

3 ______________________________

____

4 ______________________________

____

5 ______________________________

____

CHAPTER 32

Social Media Platforms

Social media consist of digital tools that help users to generate share content with the public. They cover an extensive range of apps and websites. The unique concept of social media is both uncensored and broad. Some of them concentrate on link sharing and short messages. Others are created to optimize the sharing of videos and photos. Social media face fewer limitations on what to share compared to other mass communication tools like television and newspaper. The flexibility allows anyone connected to the internet to sign up for an account. The accounts allow one to share whatever content one chooses to. Hashtags and sharing of contents enable users to attach with strangers related to the topic of interest.

While social media encompass various applications and websites, the purpose of digital tools differs. Most of them start with the user creating an account by providing personal details. Once a profile is created, individuals can formulate and share information. Social media also allows users to find others to follow or comment on. Depending on the type, users may invite each other as friends or subscribe to a page. Some platforms have 'feeds' that help users to find information. Others use algorithms related to profile data to establish the content and how it appears. Feeds mostly include information from followed users and anyone who pays for their content promotion. There is a diverse combination of social media and various services to fit into several categories. Here are some of the popular types with examples.

Social Media Networks

These networks focus on linking and exchanging ideas, content, and thoughts with others with similar interests and shares. Facebook, LinkedIn, and Twitter are good examples of social networks. LinkedIn is more professional but still categorized under this segment. While they are not the oldest types, they define the scene now. These avenues started as simple services; Twitter was the platform to answer a question while Facebook was a spot to check status. Since the rise of the phone internet, these networks are hubs that alter modern life aspects. They create memories by getting a job, reading the news, and sharing a social media photo.

Media Networks

Media networks dedicate to sharing out content like videos and photographs online. Instagram, Snapchat, Vimeo, and YouTube fall into this category. These sites are ideal for lead generation, brand awareness, audience engagement, and other social marketing goals. At the moment, there is a thin line between media and social networks as the latter has integrated business pages in the platform. However, media networks defining purpose is the sharing of media. While most media posts contain posts and texts on Instagram, Snapchat begins with a video or an image. Users may opt to add captions, mention others, or make use of filters. Similarly, sites like Vimeo and YouTube concentrate on video as the medium of communication. YouTube and Instagram share a common concept in vigilant designed assets and planned missions through a specific theme.

Discussion Networks

These networks are ideal for posts that call for more in-depth dialogue amongst users. They are the oldest methods in social media and are excellent sources for market research. If done well, you can advertise on them though posts and ads should be separated. Through the comment section, users leave comprehensive responses while others can react to those replies. Reddit, Quora, and Digg fall here, although blog sites like Word Press may be included. The massive user volume in these forums shows a hunger for comprehensive knowledge.

Review Networks

Customer review networks give people a platform to review products, services, brands, and anything else. TripAdvisor,

Zomato, and Yelp are excellent ambassadors here. Through the reviews, brands can resolve issues from unsatisfied clients. Reviews are excellent guides for new ventures too. Amazon is an ideal buying experience brought about by the review section.

Bookmarking and Curation Networks

They help people learn, share, save, and discuss new and trending information. They are useful for client engagement, web traffic, and brand awareness. Pinterest and Flipboard are good exemplars. They are a source of inspiration for those seeking ideas and information. Instagram is partially classified here as it offers users an option to accumulate content and form private collections.

Blogging and Publishing Networks

These networks allow individuals and brands tools to publicize information online to encourage sharing, discovering, and commenting. They range from contemporary Blogger and WordPress networks to microblogging ones like Interactive and Tumblr, Medium, and interactive.

What are Social ads?

In digital platforms, users are more than willing to go through the conversion process. The reason they come across a product is probably through searching specific keywords. On the other hand, social ads portray images to users who correspond with the target market. The audience already knew the product but had not planned to buy it. With only a quality image and content, the client's mind is changed. According to Cyber click, Facebook has more than 300 thousand photos posted and close to 4 million shares in one minute. Twitter counts more than 500 million tweets in a day. Hoot suite estimate that in 2020, social ads will rise by 20% to $43 billion. Despite the staggering figures, there are various ways to counter the drawbacks.

Create a Distinctive Image

The social media campaign is to achieve the utmost visibility through distinctive images. A combination of sharp contrasts and bright colors like yellow and orange is one of the tricks. Individuals are quickly captivated by vivid images. Minimize filter usage to highlight presence and intensity. Ensure that all elements fit in the picture; the text should be legible and not overlapping on logos. If offering reduced prices, include them on the photo using colors that associate with discounts. Red is an ideal one for the introductory rate, with green portraying the discounted one.

Find out the ideal platform to put Your Social ads.

There are a lot of assumptions about the most excellent way to invest in social ads. Many may associate success with the large user base, but frankly, social ad's performance depends on situations. For a positive outcome, you need to analyze where to reach your audience and the type of campaign to use for the investment. Here are the reasons why you should advertise on the following popular platforms.

Facebook

Facebook is the most extensive user base online platform in the world. Founded in 2004, it has a monthly user base of around 2.45 billion. Most importantly, it offers a reliable and trustworthy platform with an exceptionally high reach. The main advantage is the detailed segmentation options and exceedingly visual. It also gives the possibility of creating demographics to real like audiences.

Instagram

Instagram is a visual platform where users are liable to view diversified posts. It was set up in 2010 and had about 1 billion active monthly users. To maximize on Instagram advantage, you should verify the best images you may want to emulate. For a wider reach, concentrate on optimizing the videos and pictures.

Twitter

Twitter initiated in 2006 and currently has around 330 million users in a month. It has an interesting approach to social ads. It allows advertisers to make campaigns based on diverse objectives like leads, app installation, or conversion. The Twitter audience platform is winning too. Do not forget to combine with a simulated intelligence item.

YouTube

Video is contiguous to traditional advertising since it started on television. YouTube takes advantage of it by telling stories that connect with the audience. The diversification makes it perfect for placing ads. It currently has 2 billion active users monthly, a huge step from when it started off in 2005.

Snapchat

This is a relatively new concept with a youthful and tech-savvy market audience. It started running in 2011 and boasts of 360 million active followers every month. Snapchat offers ads in a natural state, relaxed and fun. They have amazing and resourceful options for vertical videos. The sponsored lenses and filters give the user to play around with your brand.

Pinterest

Pinterest is mostly female-oriented and a hotspot for anything related to them. It was founded in 2010 and had an active user base of almost 322 million in a month. Topics like fashion, cooking, and weddings carry the day. Advertisers within the niche should prioritize advertising here.

LinkedIn

LinkedIn is the most extensive professional user base that attracts the corporate audience. Advertisers offering professional solutions should use the platform for the B2B marketing strategy. It started functioning in 2003 and currently has around 330 million followers.

Common Mistakes to Avoid in Social ads

Unclear Goals

Most people who advertise online do it more like a routine without clear objectives. This is the worst approach in any investment as the campaign will flop. Your fundamental step is to understand your goals and the potential the ad offers to your brand.

Assuming the Target Audience

Before any investment, you should have a transparent target market in mind. Most businesses lack this integral aspect in their ads process and work on assumptions. According to WordStream, most Instagram users are between 18 to 34 years. With this knowledge, a company may presume that the market would appreciate memes better. This does not help you in crafting precise targeting.

Buying Followers

It is against social media guidelines to purchase followers from another platform. It is an addictive venture you can always repeat when your page gets fewer followings. The solution is to rebrand your content to maintain your followers rather than on a false basis.

Choosing a Bad Tone

A brand presence on social media is subject to strict scrutiny. It requires a balance between official and casual. If you are too professional, users **may find your ad boring. Trying too much humor may not appeal to all.**

5 POINTS I HAVE LEARNED IN MY JOURNEY TO GOING GLOBAL

1 ____

2 ____

3 ____

4 ____

5 ____

CHAPTER 33

Social Media Marketing

SOCIAL MEDIA MARKETING USES media avenues to augment sales, build brands, and influence traffic growth. In other areas, it is referred to as digital marketing or e-marketing. It allows organizations to engage clients, endorse online adverts, and analyze results through methodical tools. Through various strategies, companies find ways of engaging customers and sponsoring their content. Furthermore, compared to contemporary marketing channels, e-marketing catches the attention of a broad audience. For instance, a post can attract clients, media, bloggers, stakeholders, and the public. For a positive outcome, organizations should focus their strengths on the market audience.

There are different metrics used to measure the success of digital marketing. These include customer review rates, website statements, viral rates, and return-on-investment. Popular online platforms to advertise on include Facebook, Instagram, LinkedIn, Twitter, YouTube, Snapchat, and Pinterest. While social media marketing provides a couple of benefits, it also comes along with some challenges. If by any chance, a viral post claims that particular body oil is bleaching the skin, whether real or false, the market might get affected. It might take years for the company to recover, or it might eventually close down. Hence, proper precautions should get practiced to avoid such drawbacks. To get the best in digital marketing, here are five strong foundations.

Marketing Strategy

To succeed in social media marketing, you need to come up with efficient tactics. The main focus of e-marketing is to create content that users can share with all audiences and increase sales rates. While some companies use social media to drive traffic, others utilize it for brand awareness. Despite the success with major platforms like Facebook, there are successful upcoming ones that companies should not ignore. Some of them are TikTok, Tumblr, Whatsapp, Anchor, and WeChat. Before making any investment, it is wise to combine few platforms to target all the audience. Make up your mind on the type of information you want to share. Is the content for entertainment or learning? Compile all the required information and create awareness through videos, links, or images. As your postings pick up, you can always alter your strategies to please the growing demands.

Proper Planning and Publishing

More than 3 billion people use social media in the world. To catch the attention of this enormous figure, it requires consistency and patience. By regular updating, you give your trademark an opening to get discovered by potential clients. Circulating information in the media is as easy as posting an image, video, or blog content. In comparison to personal postings, social media marketing requires an appropriate forecast before sharing. The online market thrives through accurate frequency and timing. You should plan way ahead for likable content for your audience. There are various scheduling tools like buffer-publish that can guide you in putting out your content at the desired time. Not only does it save you time, but it helps you reach your audience at the appropriate time.

Listening and Engaging

As your social presence grows, your brand will get more noticed. You will become aware of increased comments, tags, and inboxes. In some cases, some individuals will discuss your brand without letting you know. To track your digital marketing success, you need to find a way to screen these conversations. Note that any communication from your follower can either get positive or negative. With proper monitoring, you can measure the impact social media is making on your brand. Get vigilant in checking notifications across all platforms. Even if it is not possible to track down comments that are not tagged, you can use social media tools that amass all mentions and messages.

Get Analytical Data

For a triumphant impact, you need to find out how your posts are faring in the market. In any fruitful business, the figures should pile up every month. This is not about monetary rates, but positive remarks and higher traffics. The advantage of using social media is that it provides fundamental data on the figures. Buffer-analyze is an efficient avenue that helps by comparing performance across different platforms and giving detail analytical data.

Social Media Advertising

This is an adequate area that you need to venture into. Social media helps your brand to reach a broader market and to follow. With various platforms in the market, you can identify which one to display your ads on. To settle on the best, you can analyze their performance based on actual user rates. Facebook is currently leading and should be a pedestal avenue to start with. If you chose to run various social ads at once, you could use media tools to automate, optimize, process, and create bulk modifications.

How to Use Social Media Marketing

Social media is the highest growing sector in the world. The internet had managed to accumulate more than 1 billion in the first ten years of operation. From 1996 to 2005, almost one in six persons worldwide was digitally connected. Facebook made more history when it opened its doors on September 26, 2006. It managed to reach the 2 billion monthly users in 2017, but one in five in the world had already signed up by 2011. The world population has since grown to over 7.5 billion; currently, one in four people has a Facebook account. More than 62% of the planet's population is signed up on Facebook, leading to the platforms.

How to Speed up Social Media Marketing

As other platforms get invented each passing day, the stats skyrocket. Individuals are not only using them once daily but several times. Twitter, Pinterest, Instagram are other avenues that companies can exploit to engage the market. Even though these are complementary platforms, reaching the audience is not done freely. Amy Vernon, a renowned social marketing consultant, said, "One of the biggest false assumptions about using social media for marketing is that it doesn't cost money, and its fast. Like all good things, 'getting the word out' takes time." According to her, the time spent creating marketing content is more valuable than money. Here are helpful tips she suggested to speed up the social media marketing process.

Create Your Channels Early

Before you start marketing on the online platforms, make your presence known. You may wonder how to do it before the business launch. But to create suspense and keep your client's eagerness, you can start by posting anything relevant to your industry. Strive to become a source of information for your audience. You can also hook up with other interrelated providers and discuss with them anything within the industry.

Connect with Influencers

Like any other business, social media marketing requires a cordial relationship with experts within the industry. You can start by having a conversation with bloggers and journalists who specialize in your business line. If appropriate, share, comment, and read their postings. That way, they will identify when you approach them for a favor. Create time to analyze writers who write informative content and have a considerable following. Try to associate your brand with the right market.

Discover Your Audience Market

Creating relationships and networks ahead of time is vital in social media marketing. It would help if you did so by finding out the best social platform to reach your market. Scrutinize the platforms and, if possible, place your ads there to observe how the market behaves. Finding your target market via the internet takes time. It involves figuring out the people who are communicating topics related to you. Various social media tools can help you, like SpiderQube and FollowerWonk.

Contribute to the Conversation

To engage your audience, keep the conversations running. You can join discussions that relate to your brand through Google Hangouts and Twitter talks. You can also participate through trending hashtags on other platforms. When joining, choose your words well to avoid pissing off the audience. Although Facebook, Twitter, and LinkedIn are more receptive, other platforms should not get avoided. You need to understand the audience on different platforms and adjust your content to fit in. Keep off from talking too much over-promoting your brand. Instead, attract them by sharing informative and mature content. As a result, they will get interested when you have something to promote.

Get an Expert for Your Content

All the above endeavors need time and persistence. Another aspect that people forget is the budget part. In a real sense, nothing comes free in this world. Even if most platforms offer free marketing avenues, you might need someone to assist you with it. If the funds do not allow, you can do all the work alone. But as the business grows, you might consider hiring someone. Creating engaging content requires a creative mind. If this is not one of your substantial aspects, get an expert to do it for you. You may employ one permanently, but you can get one temporarily. For a positive outcome, social media marketing requires thorough scrutiny and a friendly approach to win over your audience.

5 POINTS I HAVE LEARNED IN MY JOURNEY TO GOING GLOBAL

1 ____

2 ____

3 ____

4 ____

5 ____

CHAPTER 34

How To Set Up An Online Business Such As A Website

Online companies have skyrocketed in modern times due to minimal capital and a prospect to reach millions of people. There are estimated numbers between 2 and 3 million e-commerce businesses in the world. Due to easy setups, traditional commerce has started running its operations online. The good news is that online ventures are highly scalable. You can test a business idea for some time and decide whether to commit full-time. There are diverse ways of online trade, but the popular ones are online stores, advertising, subscription, and brokerage.

We are going to mention a few guidelines on operating a business online.

Come up with A Business Idea

The first step for any business is to settle on a business idea and form a business plan. When you have clear goals and a target audience, your business will succeed. Achievement starts by identifying customer's needs and meeting them. Start by doing some market research to understand the field better, especially on the budget required. To work on a smaller budget, you can use social media to get feedback on your idea. You can also attend related events to check out what's trending in the industry. Do not forget to do a SWOT analysis to categorize your weaknesses and strengths in your plan.

Decide on a Business Name

Every business requires a short and catchy name. If you are starting from scratch, spend time brainstorming through a list of names. Trim them down to around three or four. You can launch by registering a domain name that contains keywords easy reach-ability.

Register Your Domain Name

A domain name is an important search and marketing tool that leads consumers to your site. A strong one adds credibility to your company and sets you apart from others. It also provides visibility and awareness for your brand, attracting more customers. Compared to traditional marketing, your domain never expires if you pay the low annual fees. You only register in the web hosting companies. Check its availability; if taken, the domain website will suggest others. The best idea is to match the domain as possible to your business name to make it easier for customers to find you. Focus on getting one that ends with .co.uk or .com.

Host Your Business on the Web

A web-hosting business keeps your website on its servers and makes it available for others to see it. It is advisable to pay for the hosting rather depends on the free services offered. As you grow, you can start on the necessary packages, which include custom web hosting. Carefully confirm the customer support the host offers in case you experience problems. An ideal host should provide backup services to help businesses grow. For simple websites, an account of 0.5 GB and 512 MB is enough. As you scale up, the host can upgrade your website to sustain more traffic. Most hosting companies offer 24 hours of support all over the world and should provide SSL security certificates.

Make a Business Website

According to a research company known as Clutch.co, 64% of small businesses now have websites. Currently, there are free platforms that help you make ones like Magento, Shopify, or WordPress. That way, you can create a functional website without spending money on hosting. You only need to pay for an upgraded theme that allows more features or limited free ones. The main advantage of these sites is they regularly give SEO add-ons that guide people to your website. They are also easy to learn, and you can make an attractive site easily. If you find them complicated, you can hire an expert to guide you. Concentrate on essential things like fast delivery and stock updates. Do not overuse fonts and colors; limit to one or two. Online shops require a cart option to collect payments. Alternatively, you can introduce a credit card and other opportunities for a fee. Remember to link up your site with search engines for customers to find you.

Importance of Social Media

Social media is the easiest way to increase brand awareness. New businesses have a significant advantage as consumers love what's new and upcoming. When your website is up and running, you can integrate with Twitter, Facebook, YouTube, or Pinterest to engage more customers.

What Ecommerce is all about?

E-commerce is also referred to as the internet or electronic commerce. It is the selling and buying of products and services through the internet. E-commerce is documented to have started on August 11, 1994, where a man sold a CD to his friend through his NetMarket website. From there it has advanced to other discoveries that make transactions easier. Business start-ups and large organizations have benefited in a way that traditional retail would not have managed. By 2020, worldwide e-Commerce sales are estimated at around $ 27 trillion. Currently, they are four categories of e-Commerce models. The first one is Business to Consumer (B2C), where a company sells services and goods to a personal consumer. Then there is Business to Business (B2B), where a corporation sells to another organization. The third one is Consumer to Consumer (C2C), where a consumer sells to another consumer. For example, you can post your old bed on eBay. The last one is Consumer to Business (C2B), where consumers sell to an organization. For example, you can offer your photography services for a website upgrade.

E-commerce takes different forms of transactions between consumers and organizations. They include retail, which is the direct selling of products by a company to a user without a mediator. Wholesale is another form that concentrates on selling in bulk to a retailer. There is another option known as crowdfunding, an advanced collection of funds from consumers before the product is imported into the market. Subscription is another way that allows repeat purchase of a product until the term expires or the subscriber cancels. Then, the physical product mode is where tangible items get stocked up and shipped to customers. The digital product is another form that sells licensed online templates, media, or courses for consumption. Finally, there is the service form where a set of skills get offered in exchange for some payment.

How to Use E-commerce

It is everyone's dream to open a business and watch it grow. Putting up requires more than the business name and product listings. In e-Commerce, the best idea flops if enough traffic is not directed to the site. For successful trading, you can start by researching the e-Commerce models in the market. Keep in mind that not all business structures work for all. You need to identify with various business models to decide what to sell online. For instance, crowdfunding is a wise idea if you want to make a profit without investing heavily. The next step is to create your niche for a gainful e-Commerce shop.

Most importantly, a successful start-up site should focus on specific and not thousands of products. You can start by recognizing other competitors in the market. Do not pick an overcrowded venture and avoid anything controlled by the leading brands in the market. For successful niche-ing, concentrate on one that has a big following in social media or Amazon. If you manage a few affiliate market openings, you can make a good profit out of it.

With the niche created, confirm your products and target market. You need to know who your ideal customers are to project on a brand image. Your brand has to meet the consumers' expectations. Come up with one product idea and test how the market responds to it. From there, you can register your e-Commerce brand name and business. A successful brand connects with your personality. Take advantage of your strengths to make branding easier. The next step is finalizing the business plan by putting down things on paper. Conclude on the starting budget and monthly operating costs and move to create an online shop. With a registered business, you need to list your domain name and convey relevant URLs. Choose the convenient shopping cart options for secure payments—test other features like speed, SEO features, web developer skills, and many others. Depending on the cart option you have chosen, you might pay a minimal fee of $100 for a good template.

The last step is to attract new customers to your store. You need to do that by use of keywords and search terms. The best performing e-Commerce businesses invest a lot in marketing. For a new business, you can subscribe to newsletters or pay attention to digital podcasts. Remember that as you need to increase traffic to your site, your products require the same exposure. You can create an email list and attach offers, campaigns, or giveaways. By doing so, you manage to get subscribers and traffic real quick. You can also give bloggers free products for review. If marketing in Amazon, always ask for customer feedback to expand customer respect.

5 POINTS I HAVE LEARNED IN MY JOURNEY TO GOING GLOBAL

1 ______________________________

____

2 ______________________________

____

3 ______________________________

____

4 ______________________________

____

5 ______________________________

____

CHAPTER 35

Online Teaching Platforms And How To Use Them

FOR THE PAST COUPLE of years, online learning has witnessed ground-breaking approaches worldwide, and the 21st century introduced devices that contribute to individual intelligence more than before. Statista recorded a total of $ 46.67 billion on the e-learning product market by 2016. It is estimated that by 2022, the value will go up to more than $243 billion. E-learning redefines traditional learning and allows scalability where one is not limited. Learning without a classroom setting is relaxing as students study at their own pace. Some of the platforms offer offline content. That means that no one is left behind in the brainpower journey. The catchy part of it all is flexibility, re-usable content, straightforwardness, and affordability.

E-learning is slowly catching up with contemporary studies and also becoming an income option for many. Having a virtual tutor who interacts in a personalized way is motivating and engaging. Some programs also highlight the social and human interaction aspect through the values of teaching and learning.

The introduction of gamification, a game-based approach, is exciting and winning too. Despite the high success of e-learning, it still has some steps to the mainstream. Research by Robin Defelice and Karl Kapp states that producing one-hour lessons takes around 90-240 hours. Chapman Alliance gave an estimate of $ 10,000 per hour on production costs. The figures can be outdated and differ on different models but are a guideline. The high production costs are the main drawbacks to the innovation. Let's look at some of the informative platforms in the market.

Udemy

According to the Open education database, Udemy is a large platform with over two million scholars and 13,000 courses worldwide. It allows lecturers to create digital courses on their preferred subject. They also upload PowerPoint presentations, videos, PDFs, ZIP files, and audios to formulate directions. The platform is free for scholars who may offer their courses at a fee or free. All in all, it has a professional aspect and has a lot to offer.

Podia

This is a resourceful new platform and quite enticing on design. Through it, you can handle downloads, email subscriptions, courses, payment, and statistics. The main difference from others is that you can use downloads to sell or give away. This helps in growing the audience and attaining new customers.

Open Learning

This is an easy to use platform that allows construction and teaching of course content. The social interaction amongst students is emphasized in their motto of "Experience online teaching, the social way." From their tutorials, you can learn anything from physics to baking pastries.

Help Hub

The help hub is a digital coaching website. Not only does it connect learners and tutors instantly, but it is also engaging. The good news is that you can have group sessions to post questions and get instant answers. The casual approach to learning makes it enjoyable.

Teachable

Teachable was formerly referred to as Fedora. It creates sellable content using various media and helps you to customize the brand and launch it. The platform also gives data like the learner's methodical and course proceeds.

Learn Worlds

The most exciting part of Learn World is its involving e-book maker, video device, and interactive session with the learners. The use of gamification, which is a game-based approach, motivates the learners. Learn the world is useful, especially in content authoring and marketing. It also comes with an option to personalize domains and is ideal in corporate training.

Thinkific

Thinkific mostly offers free online classes on how to create and issue out digital materials. Designed with a variety of concepts in mind, it is all-inclusive with an essential subscription. The most important thing is that they issue certificates, integrate learning tools, and follow-ups on the learner's progress. The concept of getting user feedback is essential in adding new useful features.

RCampus

RCampus is mostly used to formulate courses, assignments, class discussions, and check grades. It is also incredible in posting learning content like links, videos, and images. The avenue uses the portfolio management method to put up multiple and functional portfolio presentations for the faculty and students. This helps them to demonstrate their knowledge and skills for career advancement.

Learnopia

This is a free online teaching platform that enables instructors to devise and offer a combination of PowerPoint presentations, audios, videos, PDF files, and multiple-choice questions. Tutors can charge their courses or give them out freely. Learnopia charges a percentage for all paid courses.

Vedantu

Vedantu is a tutorial website online created in India. It is a platform where learning is through live videos with a whiteboard visual aid. The common subjects taught are Hindi, English, Mathematics, chemistry, physics, French, German, and Computer Science.

Course Craft

Course craft is a bit dissimilar from others as it changes blogs to e-courses. Most of it is text and image, an alternative to contemporary learners who opt for non-academic courses.

Eliademy

Eliademy offers the same diversification as Udemy. It also provides features like discussions, quizzes grading, and learners' diagnostic on problem-solving.

Peer 2 Peer University

P2PU is an open education platform that gives free university courses and managed by volunteers. Tutors are allowed to come up with courses in videos, documents, slideshows, and discussion boards. The learners get a personalized approach, as enrollment is limited.

Teachers Pay Teachers

This is a website where instructors freely sell their material and not a learning platform. Lectures may post lesson plans, guides, kits, clip art, and others freely or at a price. In case of any transaction, the teachers earn royalties on cash earned.

Bibo

Bibo is a solely English training platform. The Japan-made tutorial service is based in the Philippines and aims to connect scholars all over the world.

How to Use Teaching Platforms

E-learning is one type of the umbrella term "distance learning," which means any form of learning away from the traditional setup. The fact that it happens through the internet classifies it in the group. The initiation of digital classes needs expertise in design, software development, and information technology. The process is intimidating to starters and requires thorough research on competitor's products. Coming up with a target audience and creating content that meets their needs is the core goal. To avoid confusion on how to proceed, here are informative guidelines.

Define Your Goals

To launch your online lessons, you need to decide on your product's impact on the learners. Is your approach an upgrade to the four walls? Consider if you are going to teach your students on specific topics or a complete course outline. Define the financial outcome the course will bring to your company. It would help if you also described what your learners would attain after the session.

Summarize Your Classes

You can start by dividing the modules into folders and sub-folders, each containing topics and sub-topics. Remember to outline the course objective and determine the most effective approach. Coming up with a combination of contents is informative and engaging. This is handy to audiovisual content as there is more engagement. After the module preparation, launch a delivery timeline for the content. Do not forget to document them.

Create Your Online Content

This is where the real work comes into play. The process is handy, but it should not be time-consuming. You need to put all information together. Methodically, gather the content you have developed. The videos, demos, PowerPoint presentations, and manuals must be accumulated together. Organize them in a structured manner for future reference. Explicit content will carry the day; select only those aligned to your objectives. The last step is to update the materials as necessary. Sometimes you may develop a new idea from scratch for an all-inclusive prospectus.

Connect to Your Target Audience

In this step, you are over with the substantial process of creating content. Now is the time to deliver to your targeted market. You need to come up with a practical approach to maximize success. Accessibility is as significant as the content itself. If the scholars cannot get hold of the tutorials, it is a waste of time. When we mention accessibility, we refer to the learner's first stumble upon the course. Structuring the procedure of accessing the course quickly is value-filled. There are many simplified options to access learners. They include emailing the course links, embedding it on your website, or sharing it through social media. You can also add the link to the students' other products or send them as text messages. Providing the link through a chat channel is also ultimate.

Determine Engagement Metrics

Through your dashboard, you can track the progress of the purchased content by the learner. Some platforms offer upgraded sales dashboards to tutors. The panel helps assess the metrics, check course evaluation, and guide on-course improvement as you proceed. The best way to do this is to take your first students as a guide in progress. It does not matter if you face challenges in the course line; getting feedback from them will help you perfect it. Before the official launch, any hitches can pop up. If need be, you can seek assistance from your service provider. For the final product, slot in your brand and design. You can also include a short and catchy domain to give your content a professional reflection.

5 POINTS I HAVE LEARNED IN MY JOURNEY TO GOING GLOBAL

1 ____________________

____

2 ____________________

____

3 ____________________

____

4 ____________________

____

5 ____________________

____

BONUS CHAPTERS

CHAPTER 36

The Greatest People In The Kingdom Of God

In the book of Genesis, the Bible says,

> **"Then God blessed them, and God said to them, "Be fruitful and multiply; fill the earth and subdue it; have dominion over the fish of the sea, over the birds of the air, and over every living thing that moves on the earth."**

This was the first statement God made to man. It means that every person the Lord created can be fruitful, multiply, and replenish. This is not just about children; we can also replenish the earth with ideas, creativity, and new creation with books, tapes, missions, and assignments. That is what birthing is. Every human has been gifted with that.

Some book writers out there have written books that are global bestsellers. That is why people are on network television. You can think about your favorite actors and how they can act like no one else can. The big thing airing now is these basketball players show that is on one of the network televisions, and that person can put a ball in a hoop. They are just good. That is their gift and ability, and through that giftedness, they have produced billions of dollars.

Know that your giftedness, calling, ideas, and creativity will produce greatness in influence and wealth. Giftedness attracts wealth. You pay a heart surgeon based on his or her giftedness. A CEO of an international company is paid based on that. You pay everyone based on his or her giftedness perfected. They pay Michael Jordan because of his giftedness. They pay Tiger Woods because of his giftedness. Tom Cruise is paid because of his level of giftedness in acting. You do not have to be born again or even belong to any religion before you can be gifted. If you have perfected your gifts and skills, you have packaged your branding.

Many people can play the saxophone, millions of them around the world. Nevertheless, you know who comes to your mind when you think of a wonderful saxophone player. It is even possible you can take any person and match them up with that individual. They can play just as well or better, but they have branded themselves; they have recreated themselves and have gotten into certain areas. You could think about books on leadership; who comes to mind? This is because they branded themselves that way.

Moreover, you have not branded yourself that way. It takes a change of mindset. Therefore, the first foundation is that you can innate in you to be fruitful, multiply, and replenish.

When we pray to the Lord, we do not ask him what he wants me to do. We ask him what he does not want us to do. Praise God! We want to get you to a point where when you pray, you are not praying, "Lord, what should I do? Should we go and pray? Should I write a book? Should I do that CD? Should we start the international ministry? Should I start ministering on Facebook live? Should we start teaching on global television? Oh Lord, should I start that feed the hungry center? Should I go into that new business in a time of crisis? Should we launch that work?"

We do not want you saying that. You are blessed with giftedness and fruitfulness. You have to ask, "Lord, what don't you want me to do?" Please tell me not to do these things." This is because He is pouring so much into your spirit. Do you know that you are multiple streams of blessing? However, we need you to change your mind and see yourself as that. Be fruitful.

The next point is, increase your influence. The way to start is to start at home. Before you can go global, you should have maximized your local environment. Jesus said, "Go into Jerusalem, Judea, and then the outermost part of the Earth" (Acts 1:7). Until you are faithful in little, do not desire to have more cities.

Most people that we talked with want to go global. They want to talk about, "Oh, I'm global. I have an international ministry; I have an international bestselling book." Well, that is good, especially with the internet; you can go viral on the internet in minutes. The challenge with this is the ability to sustain influence. Most of the people we have seen went viral and hit one million or ten million views, but a month after, they have nothing else to give. It was a one-time thing. You do not want to be that. You want to be someone, even if consistently, people buy your books monthly, follow your ministry, buy from your organization, and consult you. You could be a consultant at this time: a women's consultant, a man's consultant, an advisor.

There are people around the world who are looking for advisors and consultants on every topic, and some of these topics are what you know and even know so well. Start at home. Our spouses should hear most of our messages first. This is because we teach it to our family first. The Lord is more concerned about you perfecting your message at home. Your message has to be you. Your influence should start from your home.

We often challenge each other to make sure we teach publicly is what practices at home. It is always important to go home first. Get your books and write your ideas with your spouse. Start from home. That book you want to write, that CD, that song, that organization, and that business you want to develop, run it by your spouse so that they know it. They know the ins and outs of that organization before you launch it. Practice your sermons with your family. Practice your grand finale speeches with them. Perfect your delivery at home so that when they call you as the key motivational speaker before hundreds, you will remember you have your family's support.

After Jerusalem, which was the home, the next is Judea, the city. Once you have won influence over your home, you can move to your city. You must influence your city before you can have it worldwide. Then after you have gone to your city, you could speak to your nation. Now, are you perfect? No, it is not that you are perfect, but the fact is, you have perfected your message, which is your life's message. Then you will have perfected your family, inner circle, all of your friends know who you are. All your friends can be called upon anytime and know your sincerity and integrity. Your neighbors should know you. Your city should know you. What can the people in your community say about you? If you do not have such a reputation, do not push to go global yet. Stay, clean up your name. Spend at least the next three to six months. Let people see a new and changed you.

Many people have gone viral and international on these platforms, but then they get out there, and the skeletons and scandals come out to destroy them. When you get into the spotlights, the invitations and the money will keep coming. We have had money offered to us for so many things; if we did not have integrity in our community and nation, the money would have destroyed us. If we were looking for just numbers, "Likes," and followers live, we would have said all kinds of messages just to go viral.

When you come out global, you need to have high integrity because you come from one culture and going to another culture in a country like South Africa, Nigeria, Kenya Malawi, Sierra Leone, and Pakistan or to Eastern Asian, for example. Your integrity is not the same as your country or your nation. When you go to those places, money and value are different. Now, if you have a message that is just for your local community, fine. However, the truth is, for some of you, your calling is bigger than your nation. See, for the last 20 years, Dr. Collie's personal call has been bigger than his nation. We have gone to other cultures, and I have seen different value systems.

In addition, the things that we value here, in the church or business, are different, and this stretched us. If you are going to be global, many things will stretch you. Show your integrity. Show your character. Show your ability to maintain value.

God will have you on a level for a season for people around you to appreciate, honor, support, and receive the anointing, wisdom, and instruction from your life. When that period is over, God begins to ready people around the world for your calling. He readies people for your message, for your ministry, for your mantle, for your business, for your organization. The book He has placed in you to write is not only for you; he has people lined up to read that book. He has people lined up to listen to that CD. He has people lined up with that invention. He has people lined up for that cure. He has people lined up for that legal consultation. He has people lined up, and He desires to use your life to structure their lives.

He has your life lined up to be that life coach, special advisor, or confidant. We thank God for the privilege to be a confidant for leaders in every area of life: judges, police, medical practitioner, political leaders, and governmental leaders around the world. It takes the integrity of your heart and mind, and it takes knowing that God has called you.

You could be living in a small community. The way Jesus walked the earth and people saw Him. People look at you, and they see the outward appearance, but they do not know what God has placed in you to transform the world. Moreover, if you are stuck in your local church, community, or family, and you let them define who you are, you will miss your global impact on thousands of lives. If you do not come into the fullness of who you are, there will be a hindrance to the blessings of thousands of lives being blessed.

Another thing that destroyed many people is competition. The world is big enough for your audience. There is still a world of 7 billion people, and half of the world has not even heard the gospel of Christ. Not only that, there is a world of 7 billion people, and more than 6.99999 billion of them have not heard about you yet. However, we are so stuck on the bishops, the doctors, or the leaders we see on this pedestal that we never think we can make an impact. We are not in competition with anyone. We have never been, and we never will be, and you should never be either. Every time we get up, we say, "Lord, there are 7 billion people. There are over 190 nations on the Earth." That is what drives us because we want to go to the entire world. This might not drive you. The Lord might have put 10 leaders, 10 nations, or a nation in your heart. For us, God sent us to the nations. Some of the leaders of our nations might not understand it or like it. It does not matter; if they call upon us, we will support them. But I do not waste too much time with that. That is not my assignment. Furthermore, the grace on our lives is apostolic, not pastoral or bishop. It is an apostolic assignment, so we cannot focus on any one nation.

When you want to go global and make a global influence, Jesus said, "Greater works shall you do." We were not intimidated to go into nations and lay hands and release the apostolic grace, raise those people up, and now they are doing great works. People do ask, "When are you going to bring those leaders from Africa and Asia and North America and the Middle East here?" The answer is, "No, they're not going to fit here." That is not their mission. That is not their mantle. That is not their mandate.

Every time you lay hands, impart, or mentor someone, they go and duplicate you. We have duplicated over 1000 times. To the glory of God! We lost count. We laid hands on so many leaders in so many nations and sent them forth as apostles, prophets, and 5-Fold Leaders. We have duplicated ourselves. That is why we do not compete with anyone. We have replicated ourselves, so we do not compete with anyone in this city, nation, or in the world when we come here. We have planted seeds in places we cannot even go.

Jesus said, "Greater works shall you do." (John 14:12). Jesus was not intimidated as a leader to duplicate his life in twelve others. He walked with twelve disciples for three and a half years. Jesus did not raise them to become like Him alone, but to also go and raise disciples around the world. Discipleship has nothing to do with Christianity. When people read our books or listen to messages, they become our disciples.

Jesus said, *"Go therefore and make disciples of all the nations."* (Matthew 28:19). We have disciples in business, medicine, and ministry. You need to have the mindset to raise people in different spheres of influence. The statement of Jesus to us to go into the world and make disciples of all nations is the first commandment of global leadership.

We will not raise people to depend on us, but to stand on their own and have global influence. Jesus did not say, 'Please, make your ministry global. Please make your business organization global. Please make your nonprofit global. Please make your trade global. Please do international business" No. This is the command, *"Go into the world."* The world means every system of man. The word *"world"* comes from the word *"cosmos."* It is different from the word "*tierra,*" which means, "go into all the Earth."

For instance, when we travel from here to New Zealand, we are going into the earth. When we get there, we are taking the gospel into the world. The world means the system of operation, the people, or the organizations. The field of health care, law, accounting, and other fields of human endeavors constitute the world. These fields have certain practices, integrity, and code of conduct. When we got this revelation, we became global, and we have never stopped or turned back. Every field is an avenue to reach out to people. Many people do not even know we still practice medicine every single day. Even though Dr. Collie practices medicine every day, not only in a private setting but also as a consultant to the government, He is still on media platforms. We are still into book writing, we are still publishing books, we are still in business, my wife and I still have business ventures, we still read, we still do leadership training, we still do school of ministry, and many other things. We still have a family.

There is the world of economics, the world of finance, the world of media and technology, the world of religion, and the world of law. We do not have to be lawyers to know the world of law. We know enough for our function on earth. In addition, we know enough so that when we speak to a lawyer, we know how to share the gospel with him or her. Even though Dr. Collie is a physicians and Shallaywa has an MBA, we know how to speak the account's language to an accountant. We know how to speak the language of economists. In this hour, you will have to recreate to go into the world. Apostle Paul said, *"To the weak, I became as weak, that I might win the weak. I have become all things to all men, that I might, by all means, save some."* (1 Corinthians 9:22 NKJV).

When we win people in the professional world, we have won them and won their influence. Influence is more important than money. When you win people's influence; you can win them to Christ. This is another principle: To go global, you must win people's influence. Most of the places we have traveled, the invites we have gotten, speaking engagements and consultations are because we have won people and won their influence.

You need to win influence so you can win the world. You need to win their influence so that you can influence people through them. Jesus was very influential, which is why He could give us the commission to influence the world. Go into the systems and make disciples. You are the teacher, and nations are your students. Jesus sent you to 'teach all nations.' We do not care if you are white or black; Hispanic or Indian; you can teach nations.

We have sons and daughters in every race, color, and tribe. We have partners and followers in every race, tribe, and color because we do not see skin color when I see them. We do not see an economic stance or position. We see them as students, and us as teachers. That is a great responsibility. As a teacher, you have to know more than the students do. The only way you can be a teacher is you have to know more than the students do.

If you do not know more than the people who follow you, you are the student, and they are the teacher. In most ministries and organizations where the person knows more than the leader, they either suppress them or oppress them because they know the people know more than they do. However, because we know the call to discipleship, anyone who knows more math or business-like economics more than we do, we sit down and learn from them. Therefore, we learn what they know, and then we go and study online.

Suppose someone knows more scripture than us, we should give ourselves to study the Scriptures more. As a leader, it is my responsibility to lead even in my study life. It is the leader's responsibility to lead, and much more to be ahead. No one should learn more than we do, and if by any means someone knows more, we sit down and learn and hear what he or she have to say. Before you can go global, you must demonstrate good knowledge and understanding in different areas. There are some people on social media platforms who open their mouths to talk about what they have no idea of. You can tell they did not study. They did not spend any time in the presence of God. They have no life experience, and they are just coming on babbling. We cannot listen to them. Then some good people teach new things.

We get to learn a new aspect of prayer, a new aspect of worship, a new aspect of a business, a new aspect of money management, or a new aspect of wealth creation. We take that and put it into our machinery of life and life experience. We would have become a better version of ourselves. People in the world are only looking for people who know more than they do. Make a note of that. No one pays people who have nothing extra to offer. We will not pay for any course from anybody who does not know more than what we know.

If you are going to know more than what people know, you have to study more. You have to repackage your message better. You have to brand it with your idea. As an example Dr. Collie once took and online course and after teachings over telephone conversations, he went to research more because he needed to know more. If you are in an organization, and you know more, you will become a threat to them. May people may hate you because you know more. People do not hate you if you know less. You do not threaten people if you know less than they do. People are not threatened and angry if you do not seem to know more than they do.

There can never be two teachers in the same room. There can only be one teacher, and the rest disciples or students. Whenever the people we mentor becomes mature enough, like Jesus, we release them. Sometimes, I try to hire them to a greater level of responsibility, whether in the organization, workplace, foundation, or ministry work. We try to give them a greater role, so they continue to grow and give them more opportunity to learn under us. The teacher who is making disciples must always see the different levels of disciples. A disciple will begin to rise up. You must bring them up to that place. We know some people, who have been in some ministries, and they have been apostles for 20 years; they cannot tell you, one disciple they have raised. They have 500 members but no disciples. If they were to die today, there is no one to take up their position. We have seen leaders in this country, and other countries who have died and their ministry almost closed down because they did not have any successors, not one.

You are not supposed to have one. Jesus said, "Go and make disciples of all nations." You are supposed to have people around the world. Most people have organizations, ministries, churches, or groups that have no one else who sounds like them if anything happened to them. We are not talking about followers, but disciples. The church has too many followers but no disciples.

For discipleship, we call you once a week to see how they are doing. We have trained them so well, and do not need to chase after them. In fact, we try to ask you how many people you have won for Christ. How many people have you led to the Lord? How many people have you disciple? How many families do you minister to? We do not have to do all of that. That is why most of the pastors and leaders of organizations burn out. This is because they have not raised disciples. They want all the power for themselves. Either the global pandemic has shut down the world to a place where people will make disciples, or people will leave ministries and organizations, because there are too many teachers online. They are listening to their messages. They are becoming better informed and enlightened. The little buttermilk messages will not sustain them. They will desire the sincere milk of the word of God.

Make disciples. Make students. If you know how to cook, you have 50 people to teach cooking. If you do art, teach 50 people. We have discovered something about having disciples - you empower people's lives, and they are going to pay for it because you know more than they know, and they want what you have.

If you want to be a global cook, you will need to write a cookbook or do a cooking series; you have to love the people. You cannot lead or serve people you do not love. Love is a powerful drive toward going global. Love your church, your ministry, your pastor, and everyone, but rise up to your calling because you have every opportunity. Your family and life are going to be very dependent on it. You have to recreate jobs, recreate and repackage your brand for income either for yourself or for your family's future.

You must have an internal mechanism that propels you to greatness. There is greatness in the kingdom. Next, have an internal drive, an internal government. Luke 4:43, Jesus said, *"I must preach the kingdom of God to the other cities also, because for this purpose I have been sent."*

What is your sent message? Jesus knew that he must preach the gospel of the kingdom to other cities. He had a clear understanding of why he came and what God sent Him to do. There are so many messages. Many people teach and share so many things about what Jesus said and all He did, but we must not relegate His scope of assignment.

Good students always follow what their teachers left for them. Now, the student-teacher relationship back then was different from now. In those days, the mentees surround their mentor always. His disciples were always with Him. That was a common thing for persons in that time of civilization. Plato, Aristotle, Socrates, and others gathered in colosseums. These scholars taught people ideologies and teachings. Jesus with his twelve disciples following him, and then the crowd following him everywhere he goes was not a strange thing. That was how mentorship took place.

Jesus said, "I must preach the kingdom of God." The minute we package every single ministry, business, and organization to a kingdom purpose, God opened the doors for us to go global. You know people are struggling to go global because they do it in the flesh. They do it in their ability and mindset.

Before you can go global in anything you do, you have to believe you are global. You have to develop your mission, message, mandate, meat, motivation, motto, found who your mentors are, and you are ready to mentor others. Jesus remains our model when it comes to influence, multiplication, and fruitfulness. You have to be fruitful, multiply and replenish the Earth, change the mindset, love people, and have an internal government.

We teach on the Kingdom because we spent time with our mentor, the greatest one, Jesus, and we began to study every word Jesus said in Scripture, everything He said about every problem, and every answer He gave as a solution. We became His disciples and His students, and still are. We packaged ourselves according to His model. You watch Kingdom Apostolic today, and the kingdom is preached, and the Lord opens the doors. When we travel to nations, the people call and say, "Come, bring this kingdom message to this nation, come to this television station, come on this radio station, come we need your books, we want your tapes, come tell us about this kingdom."

The kingdom is not something mystical. Sometimes, it is just showing people love, and they feel the kingdom. Sometimes it is just to tell them, "Jesus loves you," and they feel it. Sometimes it is about praying to heal them and that they know Jesus loves them. Sometimes it is in the ministry of deliverance, and it is without borders. We do not have any borders that restrict us because there is no restriction in the spiritual realm.

You must have a clear drive of what you are called to do, and if we were you, we would package it after Jesus. We hear so many messages online, and they do not have anything to do with the kingdom. All of these things are going to pass away. The Bible says, "Your kingdom is an everlasting kingdom, and your dominion endures forever." (Psalms 145:13)

The things we do is kingdom related and kingdom affiliated. We are affecting nations, city, tribe, one by one, nation by nation, tribe, and language. If we cannot get there, we empower others to go there. Every time it is done, the Lord says, "It's recorded in heaven in your name, son/daughter." Get some things recorded in your name. Begin to duplicate yourself, replicate yourself in these next few months by the grace of God. We do not know how you are going to do it. Pray and ask the Lord.

Do you want to know what we did? We looked for people. Some people who are not apostolic, we found them. We reached out to some of them and said, "We want to mentor you." We saw the gifting. You need to call some people and say, "We want to disciple you. We want to mentor you. We want to take you under my wing. We want to train you in the things of the kingdom so you can even do greater."

It is good that you have a degree. Your life is worth more. We can say we have a degrees, a private medical practice, business owners, and we can list some things. Our greatest thing is our family. Nevertheless, we have made a kingdom impact in the lives of people around the world. That was what drove us. When we get to eternity, and we stand before our Master, Jesus, we will not hold hands. We love each other, but we have individual assignments to fulfill. We also have the assignment to help each other fulfill our assignment too."

Husbands, your assignment is not to be the bishop and your wife be in the background sitting in the pew with a big hat on. The devil is a liar. Your wife is supposed to be usable. She should complement you, even in the assignment God has given you. You should also support her in the things God called her to do.

When we first met her, Shallaywa did not know how to talk. Now she is preaching and teaching longer than I. I had to disciple her into the things of the kingdom. She is one of my disciples.

Husbands, disciple your wife and children in the things of God; let them be the first partakers of the grace and goodness of God in your life. As a woman, if your husband is yet to be saved, you have to disciple him until he rises to be the priest, and then he can start to disciple you. The people you went to school with could be your disciples. Your neighbors and coworkers are your potential disciples.

I remember working at the hospital; I went there and took people there as my disciples. I impacted them for about 10 years. They did not even know they were being made disciples. I shared the gospel by living it, even when it hurt. I had to live the gospel because I know they are my students. If you're going to stay on top of your global influence, always remember you're the teacher, and people are watching your life more than what you say. So, when I stepped in there, I said, "Lord, give me the strength. I am these people's teacher. I'm here to disciple them." They're watching what I eat, what I drink, how I talk, how I respond, whatever I do, who calls me, who comes to visit, you will be surprised to know. Not all of them might come to acknowledge that they follow your life, but the truth is, they are following.

Even on these social media, people are watching. They may not comment, but they are being made disciples by the teachings.

5 POINTS I HAVE LEARNED IN MY JOURNEY TO GOING GLOBAL

1 ____

2 ____

3 ____

4 ____

5 ____

CHAPTER 37

The Kingdom And Greatness

When it comes to greatness in God's Kingdom, there are principles to it. Jesus talked about greatness in a few scriptures. The Bible says,

> **"Whoever therefore breaks one of the least of these commandments, and teaches men so, shall be called least in the kingdom of heaven; but whoever does and teaches them, he shall be called great in the kingdom of heaven." (Matthew 5:19 NKJV).**

He did not say if you shout or pray, it will make you great. You could pray, dance, or even shout; none of these makes for greatness. According to the passage above, you shall be called great if you do and teach the commandment. When you are great in the kingdom of God, God will make you great in the sight of man, even if they do not like to acknowledge it. Abraham was so great that his enemies knew he was great. David was so great that his enemies knew. Moses was so great that his enemies knew. When you are great in the kingdom of God, your enemies will recognize it. Satan will recognize it.

God wants to bless you, richly, but you need to create a channel. You should have something to offer if you are looking forward to God's blessing. Use your gifting. We had always wondered why men and women of God who lived and practiced the Word and taught people were so blessed and global. We kept trying to figure out how to get my books and tapes international. How do we market them? Do we pay $1,000, $5000, get flyers and ads, and push it all over the world? No. All the stations we are on, it was one phone call, and people said yes, you bring the kingdom access. Greatness in the kingdom is doing the commandments of the Lord and teaching others to. You could use your shyness as an excuse, but you will have to obey the Lord. The first we remind ourselves of is, "We're going to live this." We do not care for the likes (popularity). To be great, Jesus said you have to do the commandments. We study together, ensuring we both meet up with the standard of the truth.

The Lord said, "Just do my commandments, follow my word, listen to people who are telling it to you, and then I will raise you up to teach it. I will make you great, and I am going to open up doors for your life in Jesus' name."

The Bible says, *"Seek he first the kingdom of God and his righteousness and all these things shall be added."* (Matthew 6:33).

We do not pray for money; we pray for the kingdom of God to manifest in our lives.

We say, "Holy Spirit, let your kingdom revelation come through us." So, all of a sudden, while praying, the Holy Spirit said, "Here's a message, tell this to the world."

Those songs in you are not for you; it is for the world. Do not rob God's church of the songs. Do not rob the world of cures. When growing up, Dr. Collie had some religious people who told me not to go into medicine. He now rejoiced and is glad that he obeyed the Holy Spirit and his gifting and calling. Because, he has touched thousands of lives to the glory of God. There is more influence in the medical field. Some people call for him as a physician who would not call a pastor, and he is a pastor. Some do not know him as a pastor, but they call him to speak to children, organizations, corporate bodies, their families, youth, school, and colleges. They would not call pastors because they do not want a spiritual perspective on the expertise.

He has spoken and prayed with more patients than on any other platform in the church at any time. If you are a lawyer, accountant, or mechanic, your clients are your disciples.

Jesus said, "Greatness in the kingdom is doing and teaching." You have no excuse whether you are a soul winner or not. We have so many manuscripts to write, and we have them lined up to publish right now. This is because we have got to disciple the world on so many different topics. Then we have songs to produce. Not being songwriter, we have songs the Lord gave to us, and we want to tell the world. There are training sessions that we have to do. We want to do and teach so we can keep being great. Greatness in the kingdom cannot cease unless you stop doing and teaching God's Word. You have to keep being great by teaching and doing the commandments of the Lord.

Another point to greatness in the kingdom is in Matthew 11:11. Jesus said, *"Verily, I said unto you, Among them that are born of women there hath not risen a greater than John the Baptist: notwithstanding he that is least in the kingdom of heaven is greater than he."*

Jesus said John the Baptist was amazing. This man baptized Jesus. Jesus submitted to be baptized by John, who was the senior prophet at that time. With the understanding of the divine order, Jesus came to submit to John. Even though John was preaching and teaching, Jesus did not start his full-time public ministry until he went to John. John saw who he was, and John said, "You're greater than me." Jesus said, "I know I'm greater than you, but you're the one with the established authority for this season, but when you baptize me, then I will come into my fullness."

You might have to meet with your mentor to release you. Notice Jesus never came out of a relationship with John. He still loved him. He was the prophet, and Jesus was the apostle. They were cousins. They were family. They grew up together, but He knew who he was in the Spirit. John Baptized Him, and not long after, Herod cut off the head of John. When Jesus got the message that John was beheaded, and they buried him, He began preaching.

Although no prophet was greater than John was, you are greater than he was. If you belong to the kingdom of God, you are so great to the Lord. Not only that, when Jesus was ready, the teacher was ready to impart the anointing on the disciples; what did he tell them? "Come, let me wash your feet." Peter said, "No, Lord, you can't wash my feet." Jesus said, "If I can't wash your feet, you can't be my disciple. You cannot go and do greater works because I am the teacher now. I am getting ready to leave. I have to serve you, into your purpose that will be greater than me, and I'm going to be off the scene." Get ready to serve some people into their greatness. You are greater than John the Baptist was.

Another point to greatness is this:

> **"At that time the disciples came to Jesus, saying, "Who then is greatest in the kingdom of heaven?" Then Jesus called a little child to Him, set him in the midst of them, and said, "Assuredly, I say to you, unless you are converted and become as little children, you will by no means enter the kingdom of heaven." (Matthew 18:1-4 NKJV)**

From this passage, you will see the power of humility when it comes to greatness. If you want to go global, you must be humble. When God raises you, you must be very humble.

When God makes you a bestselling author, bestselling CD producer, a global ministry, global minister, business man/woman with people who look up to you and honor you, sometimes when God raises you, He will demand that you do not tell anyone. He might not want to draw attention to you yet. It takes great humility to go to nations.

We had to leave everything, the comfort of our home, and go to nations and serve in places. Most folk we know would not even dare to go because it took so much breaking and humbling. In places where God breaks and humbles, you are where the oil of God flows. It is where favor, goodness, and greatness of God hide.

Jesus said when you do something like that, when you feed the hungry, clothe the naked or give alms, do it in secret. Do not do it in public. However, if you do it in public, you have your reward. We sit back and say, "Lord, no one told these pastors, bishops, apostles, prophets, prophetess etc., what not to do- because they're losing their reward?" However, the Lord said, "No, they're too high and mighty and too prideful, and people have idolized them in such a way that no one could correct him."

[As a side note]

When you do giveaways, you can send a text to people. By the time you get there, you will have enough crowds. If you want to do it in the kingdom way, you don't need a camera. This brings embarrassment to the kingdom of God. Jesus has taught us that when we give alms, we do not need publicity. When you give alms to people and bring in a cameras, you only embarrass them. When you give, you are supposed to give in private.

When you humble yourself, God will exalt you. He will bring you to the forefront, and you will be running away from the public eye because you have so much influence. Additionally, You do not need to do ads, and flyers and every day Facebook showing what you eat, what you drink, where you went. Come on, man, not for the Kingdom. That is for the world. It is a compet-itive spirit. Trying to do things for public approval is nothing but a show-off. Many people who show off their affluence on social media are in misery. They are

> unhappy and unfulfilled. That is what the Spirit of the Lord showed me for Christians. They compete with wealth, designer wears, and massage their egos with their achievements, but Jesus said that is not it. You do not become great by flaunting it. Humble yourself as a child.

Outside of a pulpit, many preachers are not great. Some people are not great outside of music playing in the background, shouting, and people cheering them. Outside of the motivation for money and getting a seed offering, most people are not great. They cannot sit down to disciple, raise people up into their greatness, send them forth, and cheer them on as Apostles and Pastors do - they father people, they birth them in the Spirit, they cheer them on, and they release them to be great. Many do not do this. Their greatness is being the Bishop, Archbishop, Apostle, and Chief Apostle, and they and their families keep rising. They have not raised or replicated their greatness in people.

Another pointer to greatness in God's Kingdom is in Matthew 20:25-28 (BSB). The Bible says,

> **"But Jesus called them to Himself and said, "You know that the rulers of the Gentiles lord it over them, and those who are great exercise authority over them. Yet it shall not be so among you; but whoever desires to become great among you, let him be your servant. And whoever desires to be first among you, let him be your servant. And whoever desires to be first among you, let him be your slave – just as the Son of Man did not come to be served, but to serve, and to give His life a ransom for many."**

In other words, Jesus said, "the world and sinners get great by riding the backs of people. Sadly, we see this in many of our religious organizations. They become great by stepping on others to get to the top. They become great by using people's gifts, callings, and abilities to promote their kingdom while not allowing others to come into their fullness and express greatness to touch the world. Jesus said the Gentiles, the sinners, and the heathens do this. However, in the kingdom of God, if you are to be great, you must be the servant.

As a single young man, I asked God, "God, how do you use my life?" I started the work of the Lord; He started using him to teach and preach the kingdom of God, to heal the sick, cast out devils, hallelujah, to travel, to write books, and then all of a sudden, I became favorable –to the glory of God! Then God added Shallaywa to my life so that we can labor together in bringing the gospel to the nations of the world. We made up in our minds to be great in the kingdom, which means we must be the servants.

How do you become great in the Kingdom? You become great when you choose to serve rather than be served. The more you serve, the greater the anointing and call upon your life. Years ago, I made up in my mind to affect all of the nations of the Earth. That was the call of God. All of a sudden, without me, pushing, manipulating my way, trying to get close to some pastors or leaders, trying to give the biggest tithe and offering, or trying to fancy my words up and be eloquent in speech, God began to open doors. He began to have people call from nations for us, and we began to go into these nations to serve people, pray with them, minister to them, and ordain them, commission them, raise them up, send them forth, and build covenant relationship with them.

You ought to be the servant, you must humble yourself as a child, and you must seek to see people you can influence. You must seek to fulfill the Abrahamic Covenant, which is; that all the nations of the earth shall be blessed through your life.

Go into the entire world, not your current country only. That place would be too small for the greatness in you. The US is not enough for you. I said, "Lord, give me the unreached nations. Give me the Middle East. Give me North-East Africa. Give me Southeast Asia. There are almost 200 nations on the earth. They have been talking about Uzbekistan and Kazakhstan. We went to Bhutan land, Madagascar, and some other places.

When we started seeing unreached nations pop up on TV, I said, "Lord, we have not even started the work of the kingdom yet." You could go for Kingdom missions in Iran, Iraq, Qatar, Doha, Dubai, Ethiopia, Egypt, Suriname, Sri Lanka, Bhutan, Nepal, Indonesia, Malaysia, Bangladesh, Philippines, Korea, Japan, and many other nations of the world. Go into the world and preach the gospel. When you go, the Lord said, "Lo, I am with you always." Every time we went into the jungles of Africa, I was never afraid of my life because I know he said, as you go, lo, I am with you always even to the end of the earth. It may not necessarily mean to travel physically; you can get on a social media platform and go! Get on an audio version and go! Preach the gospel of Jesus Christ and whatever form.

You may be interested in business, technology, electronics, social media, teaching, book writing, or platforms. Go online, and take advantage of the internet to reach the world. Use your expertise for the Kingdom and profit. When you make money, support missionary works. The work of the gospel, pastors, ministries, missionary journeys, and missionaries doing work of the Lord.

Once you surrender to the Lord Jesus Christ, give Him your heart and your life. You will be surprised to know where He will take you and all your imperfections. This season is an opportunity for you to step out. Millions are flying around hidden in opportunities, problems to be solved, online businesses, software development, electronic books, audiobooks, and even God's works. The world's employment model is changing. When you give people value, you create currents of influence. To get clients, create value. In fact, we encourage you to give value to people. Give them overvalue. Overvalue your services to them. You will gain influence, and that influence will create influence, and before you know it, there will be a current influence calling your name. Although the economy is down, your name, value, and gifting will create income channels for you. Like Joseph in a time of famine, Pharaoh is coming looking for you. You need the Holy Ghost. You need the wisdom of God. The anointing is the word of God. The revelation is by the Holy Spirit. We own nothing in this world. We are just disciples. We are not to lord it over your people but humbly serve.

5 POINTS I HAVE LEARNED IN MY JOURNEY TO GOING GLOBAL

1 ____

____

2 ____

____

3 ____

____

4 ____

____

5 ____

____

CHAPTER 38

The Leadership Secrets Of Jesus

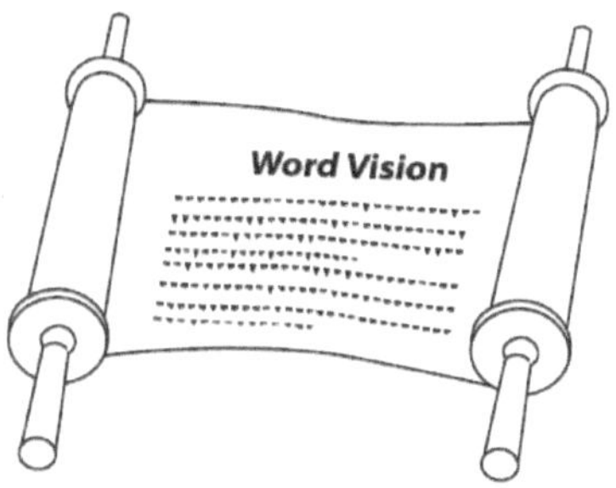

JESUS LEFT SPECIFIC LEADERSHIP instructions, whether you are a leader in the community, church, business, or ministry. Leadership is the ability to influence others to carry out a specific assignment or calling. Do you have influence? Do people call upon you to make influential decisions? Do you have the ear of others? Do you have the ears of your family, community, or the leadership in your nation?

Leadership is being upfront and the ability to influence others and galvanized people to carry out a specific assignment or calling that will bring about change. Amen! Now there is the million-year-old question: Are leaders born or are leaders created? What do you think? How many leaders are born? How many leaders are created?

Then the other question people ask about leadership. Is everyone a leader? Do you think everyone is a leader? The individual can be able to take control. Some people do not have what it takes to take control or lead; some are natural followers.

Examine the leadership model of Jesus. This model is the most successful. Over two thousand years after the death, resurrection, and ascension of Jesus Christ, He still has over a billion people; He is still powerful and still transforming people. Even though He is in heaven, his words live on. He is so powerful that He only spent three and a half years setting up His vision and people from every nation, tribe, tongue, and ethnic group has captured it. How does one become so influential although He is not physically present?

The key to true leadership is not there forever but in the continuity of your vision, words, and assignment. What is your legacy? What structures have you put in place in your leadership capacity in such a way that when you are gone, maybe not in death and maybe not in the same place, not the same position, not your vision that God can still live, still speaks?

You do not have to be in the forefront to lead. You do not have to be at the forefront of decision making. You can drive great influence and provide quality leadership from behind the scene. In the Kingdom of God, God called us to lead; He called us to be great. The saddest thing is that so many believers do not want to be great. We want to be great. Our culture, society, family background, parents, and grandparents infiltrated us with a mindset that something is wrong with being great.

There is a difference between arrogance and greatness. Arrogance draws attention to self-accomplishment, but greatness points to God. Arrogance is a fruit of the flesh and skin deep. You need to awaken your faith to greatness. Your desire for greatness is important to birth faith in you needed to shift you into that reality.

Sarah became great, although she laughed when God promised to give her a child and make her great. Greatness will come out of her womb, she laughed, and she lied that she did not laugh. God has a way of taking ordinary people through a process until they can know and enter into His promise for them. From Genesis to Revelation, He took many people through this process that makes them great. People like Noah, Abraham Moses, Esther, Samson, David, Saul, Jabez, and even the disciples went through the process that makes greatness.

He must have said something powerful for fishers to leave their means of livelihood to follow Him. These were successful people in the fishing business. However, Jesus called for a greater course; He called them for greatness beyond influence over fishes. We are called to be great.

The Spirit of God is in us; He is the Spirit of greatness. God put Him in us to bring us to a height of likeness with Him. There is greatness in you. You are not called to become God; you are called to become great like God. We have the Spirit of adoption; hereby, we cry Abba Father; it is the spirit of sonship. In the Garden, Adam lost greatness; he lost the ability to collaborate with the Holy Spirit to release greatness in the garden. Before the fall, Adam released greatness in different ways; he beautified and took care of the garden, and also named everything, and it became it. Man should cultivate the land, have dominion, possess, and multiply everything in greatness. Jesus came to save, deliver, reconcile, redeem, renounce, and restore man to greatness.

The Bible says,

> "At that time the disciples came to Jesus, saying, "Who then is greatest in the kingdom of heaven?" Then Jesus called a little child to Him, set him in the midst of them, and said, "Assuredly, I say to you, unless you are converted and become as little children, you will by no means enter the kingdom of heaven. Therefore, whoever humbles himself as this little child is the greatest in the kingdom of heaven." (Matthew 18:1-4 NKJV)

Can you ask yourself, am I great in the kingdom? Where am I in the kingdom of God? Where am I in the timing of the world's history? Where would I be in one year, five years, and ten years? What impacting legacy would I leave? What will they write on my tombstone? What will they write in my obituary?

God saw us, He saw the earth, He saw a family. He saw redemption, and He started at the end, saw the end, and went back to the beginning. You should envision your future. You must be able to see the end from the beginning of things. Great leaders, like Jesus, must learn to engage the power of vision.

Jesus used the little child to change their perspective about greatness. Stop being arrogant and prideful; become like a child.

Rule 1: Real leaders are not intimidated by bringing out the greatness in others.

Rule 2: Jesus used the opportunity to teach them something new. A real leader uses opportunities like this to teach.

> "Therefore, whoever humbles himself as this little child is the greatest in the kingdom of heaven." (Matthew 18:4 NKJV)

Rule 3: Humility is the key to greatness in kingdom leadership.

When you look at children, they believe without restrictions. To be a great leader, you have to believe unconditionally. Believe unconditionally and without restrictions. Another thing about children is that you can lead them easily. If you want to be great in the kingdom of God, you must submit to the leadership of the Holy Spirit and God's Word.

Rule 4: You must become converted and become like a child.

Children take to corrections and change easily. This is a big challenge for adults. Many people do not love corrections, and even if you correct them, they do not change easily. When a child falls and bumps his toe or scratch his knee, you will see him in the corner playing with friends in the next few moments. You must possess the ability to be flexible enough in changing situations.

Children know how to release pain and move on. A child's friend may hit that child, which leads to a fight, and when the recession bell rings, they go to the class as best friends again. They can move on from the hurt and pain. One of the limiting factors for leaders is their difficulty in releasing pain, emotional scars, and hurts of the past. You cannot be great by holding on to past resentment. Children have a better way of forgetting and letting go, but as you get older, it becomes harder to let go of things that affected you and move on. You must cultivate the habit of releasing pain and hurt that can weigh you down in the pursuit of greatness. Children can forgive more quickly and permanently. Two children may offend each other now, and in another moment, they will be out there playing as best friends again. If you want to be great, you must cultivate the habit of instant forgiveness.

We have seen into the heart of Jesus through His words as touching greatness in the Kingdom of God. Anyone who humbles himself as a child, the same is greatest in the kingdom of God. Anyone humble, broken, obedient, hopeful, and easy to forgive is an asset to the kingdom because the Holy Spirit can take such to the place of greatness. Pride is bad, and it is destroying the body of Christ. We must not take the place of God or take His glory. The Bible says,

> **"Though the LORD is on a high, yet He regards the lowly; but the proud He knows from afar." (Psalms 138:6 NKJV).**

There are things God will not share, and one of these is His glory. The Bible says,

> **"I am the LORD, that is My name, And My glory, I will not give to another, nor my praise to carved images." (Isaiah 42:8 NKJV).**

Therefore, God wants us to walk in childlike humility and openness that all we are is because of Him. All that you ever will give Him, or you have is because of Him. God can get you committed, and he will hold back nothing from you. It is nothing for God to give you a million-dollar business if you do not become proud. It is nothing for God to give you a brand-new car if you are kind enough to pick people up on the way. It is nothing for God to give you a new house on the ridge if you will bring people off the street, feed, and clothe them. There is no good thing that He withholds from them that walk uprightly. He does not want to hold anything back, but it is the state of our heart. The Lord says, "If we repent and come to humility, there is nothing He would not give us, as long as we give Him the glory.

You cannot be great if you have a spirit of pride. God resists the proud and cannot use them to minister to his people. Can God allow you to heal the sick, cast out devils, and you will not get up, go around, create cards, and start your church? If he allows you to see a miracle, you might want to start up a miracle ministry campaign. The Lord looks at the heart; He knows the heart of men. God judges intentions.

Another thing about children is that they do not discriminate. God might want to give you access to some people, but He is not sure He can trust you. Can God trust you? Can God bring people with broken lives to you for you to help and transform them?

Children do not discriminate. If you discriminate, God will not use you. Discrimination has led to sectarianism in the church. "I am of Paul," "I am of Apollo." These cannot do us any good. We are not humble enough like little children, and God says that I cannot use you because you have prejudices. You cannot be arrogant and powerful in the kingdom; it does not happen.

God will never place the man if there was not a need. The mere fact that there is a demand for you and I is because the need is tremendous. God is using people He can trust, people with a modest heart. Who are humble enough to obey him. None of us is righteous in ourselves; all of our righteousness is in Christ.

Mark 10:35-38

> "Then James and John, the sons of Zebedee, came to Him, saying, "Teacher, we want You to do for us whatever we ask." And He said to them, "What do you want me to do for you?" They said to Him," Grant us that we may sit, one on Your right hand and the other on Your left, in Your glory." But Jesus said to them, "You do not know what you ask. Are you able to drink the cup that I drink and be baptized with the baptism that I am baptized with?"

These disciples came to ask that Jesus exalt them to greatness so that they might sit beside Him in glory. Many people want to be great in the eyes of the people. They are too preoccupied with being great as bishop, pastor, minister, or leader of a church, association, or organization.

Jesus said unto them, "You know not what you asked. There is a price."

Rule 5: There is a price for greatness and leadership.

The demand for greatness makes many people drop out before even starting. Every great leader has paid the price to be great. Do you know it will also cost you? Are you ready to pay the price? Can you drink from that cup? Can you be baptized with the same baptism? Those disciples, James and John, said they could. Jesus will always give you an avenue to make a choice.

The question is, what is the cup? Can you remember the Garden of Gethsemane and the request of Jesus? The Bible says,

"He went a little farther and fell on His face, and prayed, saying, "O My Father, if it is possible, let this cup pass from Me; nevertheless, not as I will, but as You will." (Matthew 26:39 NKJV).

The cup contains suffering. The sufferings will not be the same for everyone since we have different callings and graces. The truth is, sufferings will come in different ways. You will sacrifice some friendships, relationships, and even hobbies for the sake of greatness. He might demand you let go of your boyfriend or girlfriend. He might request you chose another career path or leave your job. Whatever your cup is, when you accept the call, there will be a demand, and you will drink it.

You will go to school, experience life there. You will see oppression, and it will grieve you. You will see discrimination and injustice towards the innocent and the poor and it does something to your spirit like Jesus. That is the leadership Spirit of Christ in you. This inspires you to feed the hungry, defend the defenseless, help the helpless, provide shoes for the shoeless, and when they talk about abused children or abortion, it touches your heart. That is the leadership spirit of Christ in you.

The Bible continues,

"They said to Him, "We are able." So Jesus said to them, "You will indeed drink the cup that I drink, and with the baptism, I am baptized with you will be baptized; but to sit on My right hand and on My left is not Mine to give, but it is for those for whom it is prepared.

> And when the ten heard it, they began to be greatly displeased with James and John. But Jesus called them to Himself and said to them, "You know that those who are considered rulers over the Gentiles lord it over them, and their great ones exercise authority over them. Yet it shall not be so among you, but whoever desires to become great among you shall be your servant. And whoever of you desires to be first shall be slave of all. For even the Son of Man did not come to be served, but to serve, and to give His life a ransom for many." (Mark 10:39 – 45 NKJV).

The word "Servant" comes from the Hebrew word *Doulos*, and it means "a slave," one gives himself up to another's will. Christ used this in extending and advancing His cause among men. It means to be devoted to another to the disregard of one's interests. Jesus said if you are going to be great, you have to be the servant of others.

Many are so busy and corrupt, and they want people to serve them. The Word of God reveals that you must be willing to serve others if you want to be great. What you do in secret makes you great in God publicly. Everyone wants people to serve him or her; they want people to minister to them. According to the word of God, you will not be great that way. It is not sitting in a special seat that makes you great; it is serving.

Personally, our family often look for ways to serve. Become a slaves to God and the body of Christ. We serve because we are building Kingdom greatness. In order to be great and come to Jesus, find an area to serve and serve. There are so many battered children and so many hungry people, serve them. If the lord stirs your heart to help them in any way, do not hesitate to serve.

When you are at home, serve. Serve your parents, serve your children, serve your relatives, and serve anyone and everyone. If you want to be a leader, you must learn to serve. We have been privileged to serve men of God, and we have served together with them. Servant leadership is the kingdom's key to greatness. A great man is the one who serves. We served in the hospital at a private practice and full-time classes for seven years with the resources of people we have, and we keep applying those two principles to keep serving others and staying humble for the Lord. We have seen him exalt us in ways that no man can do, and we believe He can do the same for you.

5 POINTS I HAVE LEARNED IN MY JOURNEY TO GOING GLOBAL

1 ______________________________

____

2 ______________________________

____

3 ______________________________

____

4 ______________________________

____

5 ______________________________

____

References

"11 Ways to Communicate Better Across Language and Culture Barriers." Oxford Royale Academy, 15 Feb. 2018, www.oxford-royale.com/articles/communicate-better-language-and-culture-barriers/.

"8 Ways to Add Value to Your Life in the New Year." Sixty and Me, 3 Sept. 2019, sixtyandme.com/8-ways-to-add-value-to-your-life-in-the-new-year/.

"Creating Value." 7 Mindsets, 8 Mar. 2020, 7mindsets.com/creating-value/.

"Digital Marketing Careers at Digital Vidya." Digital Vidya, 5 Aug. 2020, www.digitalvidya.com/careers/.

"Ecommerce Definition - What Is Ecommerce." Shopify, www.shopify.com/encyclopedia/what-is-ecommerce.

"Facebook Net Worth 2009-2020: FB." *Macrotrends*, www.macrotrends.net/stocks/charts/FB/facebook/net-worth.

"How To Build a Global Mindset." Aperian Global, 3 Dec. 2019, www.aperianglobal.com/how-to-build-global-mindset/.

"Marketing News, Interviews and How-to Guides." Search Engine Journal, 31 Dec. 1969, www.searchenginejournal.com/.

"Measuring Global Mindset®." Thunderbird School of Global Management, 2 Sept. 2018, thunderbird.asu.edu/knowledge-network/measuring-global-mindset-article.

"Small Businesses." Small Businesses.com, www.smallbusinesses.com/.

"Social Media Marketing Made Simple: A Step-by-Step Guide." Neil Patel, 28 Oct. 2020, neilpatel.com/what-is-social-media-marketing.

"Spiritual Gift of Leadership." Spiritual Gifts Test, 28 June 2017, spiritualgiftstest.com/spiritual-gift-leadership/.

"The Butterfly Effect: Everything You Need to Know About This Powerful Mental Model." Farnam Street, 3 Dec. 2020, fs.blog/2017/08/the-butterfly-effect/.

"What Is Social Media Marketing?" Buffer, buffer.com/social-media-marketing.

Ashwini Murthy "How Many e-Commerce Companies Are There?: PipeCandy." Insights on the Global ECommerce & DTC Businesses, 10 Mar. 2020, blog.pipecandy.com/e-commerce-companies-market-size/.

Berry, Tim, et al. "How to Write a Mission Statement in 5 Easy Steps." Bplans Blog, 5 Nov. 2020, articles.bplans.com/writing-a-mission-statement.

Blue Corona "75+ Small Business Digital Marketing Statistics 2019." Blue Corona, www.bluecorona.com/blog/29-small-business-digital-marketing-statistics/.

Büchel, Bettina, and Michael Sorell. "The Five Keys to Developing a Successful Global Mindset." IMD Business School, IMD Business School, 30 July 2018, swww.imd.org/research-knowledge/articles/developing-a-global-mindset-the-five-keys-to-success/.

Cyberclick. "Cyberclick · Digital Marketing Agency." Cyberclick, www.cyberclick.net/.

Dan Noyes "Top 20 Facebook Statistics - Updated October 2020." *Zephoria Inc.*, 29 Oct. 2020, zephoria.com/top-15-valuable-facebook-statistics/.

DeMatas, Darren "How To Start an Ecommerce Business From Scratch." Ecommerce CEO, 3 Dec. 2020, www.ecommerceceo.com/start-ecommerce-business/.

Erin Duffin "Topic: E-Learning and Digital Education." Statista, www.statista.com/topics/3115/e-learning-and-digital-education/.

First, Reach. "What Is Corporate Branding and How It Is Done?" Reach First Inc., 28 Apr. 2020, www.reachfirst.com/what-is-corporate-branding-and-how-it-is-done/.

Henderson, Gary. What Is Personal Branding?, www.digitalmarketing.org/blog/what-is-personal-branding.

III, George N. Root. "Factors Affecting Effective Teamwork." Small Business - Chron.com, Chron.com, 8 Mar. 2019, smallbusiness.chron.com/factors-affecting-effective-teamwork-965.html.

Inc., Hootsuite. "Social Media Marketing & Management Dashboard." Hootsuite, hootsuite.com/.

John Rampton "9 Proven Ways to Gain Influence, Money and Power." Due, 27 Nov. 2019, due.com/blog/9-proven-ways-to-gain-influence-money-and-power/.

Mansoor Iqbal "Zoom Revenue and Usage Statistics (2020)." Business of Apps, 30 Oct. 2020, www.businessofapps.com/data/zoom-statistics/.

Martinuzzi, Bruna, et al. "Why Being a Generous Leader Can Make You a Great Leader: Show People Why They Matter." Mind Tools, www.mindtools.com/pages/article/newLDR_55.htm.

McCatty, Natalie. "Corporate Branding: What It Is, and How to Do It Right." Search Engine Journal, Search Engine Journal, 20 Nov. 2017. www.searchenginejournal.com/corporate-branding-right/96041/.

Open Education Database "6 Free Online Teaching Platforms: Design Custom Courses." OEDB.org, Copyright © 2006-2020 OEDb.

org, a Red Ventures Company, 2 Aug. 2018, oedb.org/ilibrarian/6-free-platforms-teaching-online/.

Pappas, Christopher. "Top 20 ELearning Statistics For 2019." ELearning Industry, 13 July 2020, elearningindustry.com/top-elearning-statistics-2019.

Parrish, Cayleigh. "How To Use Social Media To Market Your Business." Fast Company, Fast Company, 27 Apr. 2017, www.fastcompany.com/3047232/how-to-use-social-media-to-market-your-business.

Ramsey Solutions. "Using Your God-Given Talents." Daveramsey.com, Ramsey Solutions, 23 Sept. 2019, www.daveramsey.com/blog/using-your-god-given-talents.

Ray, Stephanie. "A Guide to Writing the Perfect Vision Statement (with Examples)." Project Manager.com, Project Manager.com, 30 Oct. 2020, www.projectmanager.com/blog/guide-writing-perfect-vision-statement-examples.

Rebecca Knight "How to Increase Your Influence at Work." Harvard Business Review, 3 Apr. 2018, hbr.org/2018/02/how-to-increase-your-influence-at-work.

Rebekah Carter "Must Have Video Conferencing Statistics 2020." UC Today, 28 July 2020, www.uctoday.com/collaboration/video-conferencing/video-conferencing-statistics/.

Schell, Michael S., et al. "The Importance of a Global Mindset." Training Industry, 15 Dec. 2017, trainingindustry.com/blog/content-development/the-importance-of-a-global-mindset.

Sean Peek "How to Write a Vision Statement." Business News Daily, www.businessnewsdaily.com/3882-vision-statement.html.

Seline Shenoy, et al. "5 Enriching Ways to Embrace Other Cultures." The Dream Catcher, 17 June 2020, thedreamcatch.com/5-enriching-ways-to-embrace-other-cultures/.

Sergiy Movchan "How Much Does It Cost to Develop an Online Course?" How Much Does It Cost to Develop an Online Course in 2020?, raccoongang.com/blog/how-much-does-it-cost-create-online-course/.

Simon Kemp "Digital 2020: 3.8 Billion People Use Social Media." *We Are Social*, 4 Feb. 2020, wearesocial.com/blog/2020/01/digital-2020-3-8-billion-people-use-social-media.

Team, Vantage Circle Content. "10 Reasons Highlighting The Importance Of Team Buildin." Nurture an Engaged and Satisfied Workforce | Vantage Circle HR Blog, Nurture an Engaged and Satisfied Workforce | Vantage Circle HR Blog, 30 Oct. 2020, blog.vantagecircle.com/importance-of-team-building/.

The balance careers: https://www.thebalancecareers.com/what-is-team-building- 1918270 (What is team building)

Thorp, Tris. "Self-Worth: 5 Ways to Identify Your Unique Gifts." Chopra, Chopra, 12 Nov. 2020, chopra.com/articles/self-worth-5-ways-to-identify-your-unique-gifts.

Tom. "The History of Online Education." Peterson's, Peterson's, 4 Feb. 2019, www.petersons.com/blog/the-history-of-online-education/.

Ward, Susan. "What Is a Mission Statement?" The Balance Small Business, www.thebalancesmb.com/mission-statement-2947996.

Welcome To Global Christian Leadership And Entrepreneurship

"Therefore go and make disciples of all nations, baptizing them in the name of the Father and of the Son and of the Holy Spirit, and teaching them to obey everything I have commanded you. And surely I am with you always, to the very end of the age" (Mathew 28:19-20 NIV).

The Lord is with you always and in everything you do. In this your new pursuit, may you find God in all you do, and may God find you in all He does. Amen

www.ingramcontent.com/pod-product-compliance
Lightning Source LLC
LaVergne TN
LVHW090312210926
848480LV00001B/216